$28.70

2003

THE IMPORTANCE OF

The Wright Brothers

by Michael J. Martin

LUCENT
BOOKS®

THOMSON
★
GALE™

San Diego • Detroit • New York • San Francisco • Cleveland • New Haven, Conn. • Waterville, Maine • London • Munich

THOMSON
———✳———™
GALE

© 2003 by Lucent Books. Lucent Books is an imprint of The Gale Group, Inc.,
a division of Thomson Learning, Inc.

Lucent Books® and Thomson Learning™ are trademarks used herein under license.

For more information, contact
Lucent Books
27500 Drake Rd.
Farmington Hills, MI 48331-3535
Or you can visit our Internet site at http://www.gale.com

LIBRARY OF CONGRESS CATALOGING-IN-PUBLICATION DATA
————————————————————————————————

Martin, Michael J.–
    The Wright brothers / by Michael J. Martin
v. cm. — (The importance of)
Includes bibliographical references and Index.
Contents: Will and Orv—The bicycle builders—An idea takes wing—Flight School—The
whopper flying machine—Pioneers of the pasture—The bird men of 1908—Fame and
fortune—Masters of the air.
    ISBN 1-56006-847-7 (hardback : alk. paper)
    1. Wright, Orville, 1871–1948—Junvenile literature. 2. Wright, Wilbur, 1867–1912
—Juvenile literature. 3. Aeronautics—United States Biography—Juvenile literature.
4. Inventors—United States—Biography—Juvenile literature. 5. Aeronautics—United
States—History—Juvenile literature. [1. Wright, Orville, 1871–1948. 2. Wright, Wilbur,
1867–1912. 3. Aeronautics—Biography.] I, Title. II. Series (San Diego, Calif.)
    TL540.W7 M373 2003
    629.13'092'272—dc21

                          2002005391

Printed in the United States of America

Contents

Foreword

THE IMPORTANCE OF biography series deals with individuals who have made a unique contribution to history. The editors of the series have deliberately chosen to cast a wide net and include people from all fields of endeavor. Individuals from politics, music, art, literature, philosophy, science, sports, and religion are all represented. In addition, the editors did not restrict the series to individuals whose accomplishments have helped change the course of history. Of necessity, this criterion would have eliminated many whose contribution was great, though limited. Charles Darwin, for example, was responsible for radically altering the scientific view of the natural history of the world. His achievements continue to impact the study of science today. Others, such as Chief Joseph of the Nez Percé, played a pivotal role in the history of their own people. While Joseph's influence does not extend much beyond the Nez Percé, his nonviolent resistance to white expansion and his continuing role in protecting his tribe and his homeland remain an inspiration to all.

These biographies are more than factual chronicles. Each volume attempts to emphasize an individual's contributions both in his or her own time and for posterity. For example, the voyages of Christopher Columbus opened the way to European colonization of the New World. Unquestionably, his encounter with the New World brought monumental changes to both Europe and the Americas in his day. Today, however, the broader impact of Columbus's voyages is being critically scrutinized. Christopher Columbus, as well as every biography in The Importance Of series, includes and evaluates the most recent scholarship available on each subject.

Each author includes a wide variety of primary and secondary source quotations to document and substantiate his or her work. All quotes are footnoted to show readers exactly how and where biographers derive their information, as well as provide stepping stones to further research. These quotations enliven the text by giving readers eyewitness views of the life and times of each individual covered in The Importance Of series.

Finally, each volume is enhanced by photographs, bibliographies, chronologies, and comprehensive indexes. For both the casual reader and the student engaged in research, The Importance Of biographies will be a fascinating adventure into the lives of people who have helped shape humanity's past and present, and who will continue to shape its future.

IMPORTANT DATES IN THE LIVES OF THE WRIGHT BROTHERS

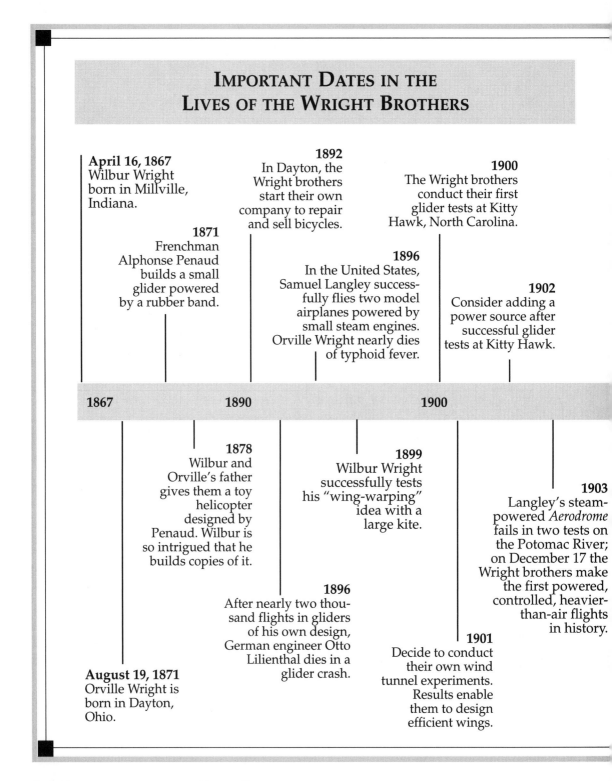

April 16, 1867
Wilbur Wright born in Millville, Indiana.

1871
Frenchman Alphonse Penaud builds a small glider powered by a rubber band.

1892
In Dayton, the Wright brothers start their own company to repair and sell bicycles.

1896
In the United States, Samuel Langley successfully flies two model airplanes powered by small steam engines. Orville Wright nearly dies of typhoid fever.

1900
The Wright brothers conduct their first glider tests at Kitty Hawk, North Carolina.

1902
Consider adding a power source after successful glider tests at Kitty Hawk.

1867   **1890**   **1900**

1878
Wilbur and Orville's father gives them a toy helicopter designed by Penaud. Wilbur is so intrigued that he builds copies of it.

1899
Wilbur Wright successfully tests his "wing-warping" idea with a large kite.

1903
Langley's steam-powered *Aerodrome* fails in two tests on the Potomac River; on December 17 the Wright brothers make the first powered, controlled, heavier-than-air flights in history.

1896
After nearly two thousand flights in gliders of his own design, German engineer Otto Lilienthal dies in a glider crash.

1901
Decide to conduct their own wind tunnel experiments. Results enable them to design efficient wings.

August 19, 1871
Orville Wright is born in Dayton, Ohio.

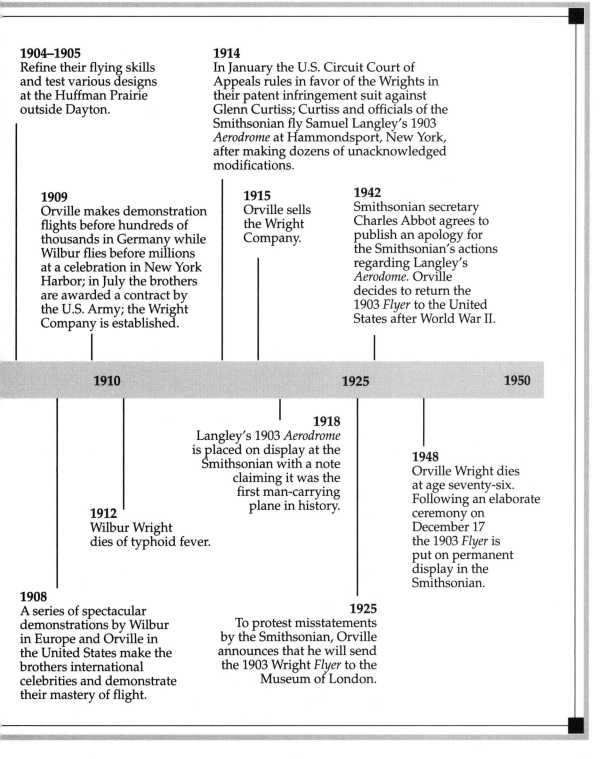

1904–1905
Refine their flying skills and test various designs at the Huffman Prairie outside Dayton.

1914
In January the U.S. Circuit Court of Appeals rules in favor of the Wrights in their patent infringement suit against Glenn Curtiss; Curtiss and officials of the Smithsonian fly Samuel Langley's 1903 *Aerodrome* at Hammondsport, New York, after making dozens of unacknowledged modifications.

1909
Orville makes demonstration flights before hundreds of thousands in Germany while Wilbur flies before millions at a celebration in New York Harbor; in July the brothers are awarded a contract by the U.S. Army; the Wright Company is established.

1915
Orville sells the Wright Company.

1942
Smithsonian secretary Charles Abbot agrees to publish an apology for the Smithsonian's actions regarding Langley's *Aerodome*. Orville decides to return the 1903 *Flyer* to the United States after World War II.

1910   **1925**   **1950**

1918
Langley's 1903 *Aerodrome* is placed on display at the Smithsonian with a note claiming it was the first man-carrying plane in history.

1948
Orville Wright dies at age seventy-six. Following an elaborate ceremony on December 17 the 1903 *Flyer* is put on permanent display in the Smithsonian.

1912
Wilbur Wright dies of typhoid fever.

1908
A series of spectacular demonstrations by Wilbur in Europe and Orville in the United States make the brothers international celebrities and demonstrate their mastery of flight.

1925
To protest misstatements by the Smithsonian, Orville announces that he will send the 1903 Wright *Flyer* to the Museum of London.

They Gave Us Wings

"How was it, how could it be that two young men from Ohio, without special training or special advantage, should succeed where all others had failed?"
—Walter Bonney, *Prelude to Kitty Hawk*

As the twentieth century began, hardly anyone believed that humans could build a machine that would fly. Most scientists agreed that the idea was preposterous. Some claimed that it violated the laws of

By pursuing their dream of flight, Wilbur (left) and Orville Wright changed the course of history.

Above the sand dunes near Kitty Hawk the Wright Brothers mastered the principles of flight.

physics. Meanwhile, the public tended to agree with the old saying, "If God had intended man to fly, He would have given him wings."

Yet, two inquisitive and inventive brothers—neither of whom had even graduated from high school—refused to listen to the experts. With persistence, enthusiasm, and quiet confidence, Wilbur and Orville Wright pursued the dream of flight. In the process, they not only figured out how to fly, they changed the world forever.

Had the Wright brothers heeded the words of authorities like John Le Conte, a famed naturalist of the day, their dreams never would have gotten off the ground.

Le Conte assured people that "a flying machine is impossible, in spite of the testimony of the birds."[1] The general public was just as skeptical. Most regarded flying-machine inventors with pity, if not ridicule.

A popular poem by John Trowbridge illustrates that most people thought the sky was no place for humans. The poem, "Darius Green and His Flying Machine," recalls the humorous misadventures of a farm boy who decides to build a flying machine that does not fly at all. By the end of the nineteenth century, the poem had been recited in thousands of schools and reprinted in countless books and newspapers. It ended with the moral, "Stick to your sphere."[2]

As Orville Wright recalled later, "Flight was generally looked upon as an impossibility."[3] But he and his brother Wilbur had an idea that this belief might not be true at all.

The date of their first flight, December 17, 1903, may well be the most important date in the history of aviation. Certainly, it was one of the greatest days of Wilbur and Orville's lives. After more than four years of hard work, they succeeded in realizing a dream that nearly everyone said was impossible.

They were now absolutely certain that they knew more about aerodynamics than anyone in the world. And, in fact, every airplane that has flown since then is a direct descendant of the flying machine they built and piloted a few feet above the sand dunes of North Carolina on that cold and windy December day.

Although it took a surprisingly long time for the world to recognize the Wright brothers' accomplishments, there is no longer any doubt about the legacy of these two humble but unusually determined young men. Not only did they engineer one of the great technological advances of all time—they helped bring about an entirely new world.

1 "He Had Much Faith in His Children"

The family of Wilbur and Orville Wright was unusual in a number of ways. Not only were the relationships very close but the children were raised to be exceptionally independent and self-confident. That background, plus the family's unconditional support, would be a source of strength when the rest of the world thought Wilbur and Orville were a couple of crazy fools.

Wilbur entered the world first, on April 16, 1867. He was the middle child of five. At the time, the family was living in Millville, Indiana. Wilbur's two older brothers, Reuchlin and Lorin, were five and six in 1867. Four years later the Wrights moved to Dayton, Ohio. Orville was born there on August 19, 1871. The family's only girl, Katharine, was born exactly three years later, on August 19, 1874.

Milton Wright, the boys' father, was a bishop in the Church of the United Brethren in Christ. As part of his job, he had to spend several months each year away

This 1915 photograph of the Wright family includes Orville (standing), his father Milton (bearded), and his sister Katharine (far right).

from home. Still, no matter where he was, he took time to write letters to his children, sharing with them the sights he had seen. A former teacher, he had strong ideas about how children should be educated.

Several of the Wright children were pupils of teacher Esther Wheeler. She had vivid memories of discussions with Milton Wright about his unusual belief that children should have a day off from school every now and then:

> The Bishop and I have clashed over that proposition many times, but he was set in his ways and could not be

---

"MUCH AFFECTION"

In The Bishop's Boys *Tom Crouch comments on the unusual closeness of the Wright family and how, in some ways, Wilbur was the odd man out.*

As the middle child in a large family Wilbur Wright often felt displaced and isolated.

"If there were occasional disagreements among the children, and a need for discipline, there was also much affection in this family. Milton and Susan were warm, loving, and protective parents, who encouraged a close relationship between their children. As in any group of brothers and sisters born over a thirteen-year period, the bonds were especially strong between those children who were closest in age, Reuchlin and Lorin, eldest sons, were particularly close, as were Orville and Katharine, the two youngest.

Wilbur was in every sense the middle child. Four and a half years younger than Lorin, he was the tag-along little brother. In high school he tended to draw his friends from an older circle met through Reuch and Lorin. He was the youngest member of a local men's club otherwise composed entirely of his elder brothers' classmates.

Four years older than Orville, Wilbur took his own responsibilities seriously. He told Orv stories, taught him to build kites, and served as an unofficial guide and adviser to his gang of friends. At the same time, he was careful to maintain a respectable distance from childish goings-on."

won over by any sort of argument. He had much faith in his children and believed that they could keep up with their classes and miss a few days also. Whether he was right in allowing them to remain away, I will not try to answer, but his boys were excellent scholars, just as he argued they would be.[4]

AN UNUSUAL INHERITANCE

The Wright brothers' exceptional mechanical ability seems to have been inherited from their mother. As a child, Susan Koerner Wright had been very close to her father. He was a master carriage and wagon maker and she spent many hours in his shop watching him work. An unusual woman for her day, Susan Wright not only went to college but also excelled in mathematics. According to family members "she could mend anything,"[5] and she also designed and repaired simple household appliances and even built sleds for her children.

Wilbur once said that, "From the time we were little children, my brother Orville and myself lived together, played together, worked together and, in fact, thought together."[6] Although "Will" and "Orv"—as they were called by their family—were remarkably alike, there were notable differences in their personalities.

Wilbur was the quiet, self-confident one, while Orville tended to be more enthusiastic. Orville raced from one project to another, throwing himself wholeheartedly into whatever interested him. As a

Orville was a vivacious youngster whose early mechanical inclination fueled his pursuit of flight.

six-year-old "businessman," he collected bones and sold them for fertilizer. Later, he built and sold kites and organized an amateur circus in the Wright's backyard.

Orville's innate mechanical curiosity was evident early on. He once skipped kindergarten to "oil" a sewing machine by dropping water into the oil holes with a feather. A letter written in 1881 describes another of his early "experiments":

Dear Father,
I got your letter today. My teacher said I was a good boy today. We have 45 in our room. The other day I took a machine can and filled it with water, then put it on the stove. I waited a little while and the water came squirting out of the top about a foot.
Your son, Orville[7]

Orville had the kind of bright, restless mind that can give teachers headaches. He learned fast and became bored easily. That probably is why teachers tended to put him in the front of the class where they could keep a close eye on him. For years, the rest of the family teased Orville about his "front-row" education.

When Orville was in the sixth grade the Wrights were living in Richmond, Indiana. One day an exasperated teacher kicked him out of class for some sort of mischief. He was told not to come back without a note from his parents.

Orville decided that his parents probably did not need to know about the matter and took the rest of the school year off. He had done something similar in kindergarten. After his first day, he left home each morning and went to play at a friend's house. Because he returned every afternoon at the correct time, it was weeks before the family realized what he was up to. When they finally figured it out, they hired a tutor for him so he could catch up with his classmates.

A BOOKISH BOY

Wilbur was far less of a trial for his teachers. One recalled that he was "too dreamy"[8] to get into much trouble. A voracious reader with a fine memory, Wilbur liked thinking things through so much that he sometimes got lost in his own thoughts. "When he had something on his mind," recalled a relative, "he would cut himself off from everyone. At times he was unaware of what was going on around him."[9]

As a youth Wilbur spent much of his time reading or in quiet contemplation.

The encyclopedia at home was a favorite book, and he seemed able to absorb nearly everything he read. As biographer Fred Kelly once pointed out, while it might appear that "Orville was into more different things at this time than his brother, it was mainly because Wilbur's great passion was for reading."[10]

Unlike Orville, Wilbur had a tendency to become moody and depressed. Like Orville, he enjoyed solving mechanical problems. He also had a knack for understanding complex ideas and explaining them clearly. For a time, he considered becoming a teacher or a minister.

Like many people who spend much time in deep thought, Wilbur was not

THE WRIGHT STUFF

Neil Armstrong, the first man to set foot on the moon, inspired pilot and aviation authority Harry Combs to look more closely at the Wright brothers and their achievements. In this excerpt from his book Kill Devil Hill: Discovering the Secret of the Wright Brothers, *Combs describes the personalities that lay beneath the Wright brothers' public image.*

"They were athletes, these two. They were fun-loving and curious about almost all things. Each had a marvelous sense of humor. How different from the dimensionless characters often found in the words written by these two men! That they were honest, decent, humble men has been said about them often enough.

But that they loved a good joke, that they were inventive in almost all things, that they dedicated themselves fiercely to family love and care, that their respect for others was so unbending that it tugged the edge of imagination—all this, and more, lay buried behind newspaper copy and their photographs.

The older, Wilbur, showed to the world a face of hawklike determination, so often unsmiling, he became identified with excessive seriousness and a tenacity that forbade the presence of humor. How should we know that he was as tender and warm as he really was behind that hawkish look—that he could retain a gentle dignity with steel behind it, a sense of humor dry and deep, that he could throw off frustrations and continue to strive when all odds were against him. . . .

Four years the younger, bearer of a mustache that hid an impish curling of the lip, was Orville. In him one could see at once the sensitive and inquiring expression that reflected an agile mind, darting swiftly from one grand idea to another."

Orville Wright possessed a good sense of humor.

overly concerned with how he looked. Often, his younger sister Katharine found herself checking to make sure his clothing matched.

Although quieter, Wilbur was more self-assured than Orville (who was shy around strangers). History was one of his favorite subjects, and he had an ambition to do something important with his life. Orville, possessed of a more practical and restless turn of mind, plunged headlong into whatever project currently interested him. He was more outgoing and playful than Wilbur with people he knew well enough to trust.

A Terrific Toy

Both boys, however, were fascinated by a gift they had received when Wilbur was eleven and Orville seven. The year was 1878 and they were living in Cedar Rapids, Iowa, because their father had been sent there after he became a bishop. One day he brought home a popular toy—a tiny flying machine powered by rubber bands. Designed by a Frenchman named Alphonse Penaud, it was a kind of miniature helicopter. Orville and Wilbur were fascinated by the little flying machine. They played with it for hours. When it finally broke, Wilbur built copies, some of them bigger than the original.

And, in Orville's mind at least, an ambitious idea began taking shape. Around this time, Ida Palmer, a teacher at the Jefferson School in Cedar Rapids, caught him at his desk fiddling with a couple of pieces of wood. When asked what he was

up to, Orville told her he was putting together a flying machine and that someday he and his brother might fly together in a larger version.

Despite Orville's enthusiasm, Wilbur's bigger versions of Penaud's toy did not fly well. At the time, the boys did not realize that larger flying machines needed much more power than a rubber band could supply. Still, their actions highlight one of the brothers' strongest traits—they loved taking a thing apart, figuring out how it worked, and then building something even better.

In June of 1884 the Wright family moved back to Dayton, which became their permanent home. Since Orville had not actually graduated from sixth grade in Richmond, the Dayton school officials insisted that he repeat the grade. Greatly upset, Orville made such a fuss that he was finally allowed into the seventh grade. It was made clear, however, that if he had the least bit of trouble keeping up, he would immediately be sent back to sixth grade. Challenges always seemed to bring out the best in Orville. By the end of the school year he had been named the outstanding mathematics student in the city.

While both brothers had an unusual ability to concentrate on whatever interested them, they were by no means humorless drones. Orville was a great practical joker who liked racing bikes, playing his guitar, and going on camping trips. Wilbur was a good athlete with a quiet sense of humor, who, as a friend put it, would rather "say something dry and droll, if he said anything at all."[11] Besides being an excellent ice-skater and fine gymnast,

Wilbur was among the faster runners on the high school football team.

A Passion for Printing

Despite their interests in various sports, by the late 1880s the Wright brothers, then in their teens, were becoming increasingly known for their mechanical abilities. After seeing some woodcut illustrations in a magazine Orville became interested in wood engraving. He could not afford to buy engraving tools, but that did not stop him. "Not having the necessary funds to purchase engraving tools," he recalled years later, "I found that the springs out of pocket knives would quite satisfy the purpose and it was with these springs, refashioned of course, that I spent many an hour at wood engraving."[12]

Noticing how much his little brother enjoyed the hobby, Wilbur bought him some real engraving tools for Christmas. Orville's interest in engraving eventually led to a fascination with printing. Not long after the family returned to Dayton, Orville was delighted to discover that an old childhood friend, Ed Sines, had a tiny printing press. Although it was really just a toy, the two boys formed their own printing company and went into business together.

They began by producing a newspaper, the *Midget,* for their eighth-grade classmates. The *Midget* lasted for only one issue, but then they branched out into making letterheads, business cards, envelopes, and advertising circulars. Orville's father helped them by sending small church jobs their way.

One of the secrets to the Wright brothers' ultimate success was that their siblings and parents always stood behind them. Orville was once asked if the family had ever discouraged any of his interests. "No," he replied, "on the contrary we were encouraged just so long as we were working on anything, no matter what it was, that remained within the bounds of reason."[13]

Orville's fascination with printing was no exception. Impressed by how hard Orville was working, Milton talked Wilbur and Lorin into trading a boat they had made for a real printing press for Orville. After they did so, Milton bought Orville twenty-five pounds of type. But the new press printed only sheets of paper that measured three inches by four-and-a-half inches.

The Joy of Building

Deciding he needed a bigger press, Orville designed and built one himself—with Wilbur acting as a consultant. Even though it was made out of buggy parts, scrap metal from various junkyards, and a damaged tombstone, it actually worked. By then printing was Orville's passion and seemed likely to be his future. During the summer he worked up to sixty hours a week at a local print shop, learning everything he could about the business.

Still, as always, he most enjoyed creating something uniquely his own. In the spring of 1888, when he was still only sixteen,

After designing and building his own printing press, Orville Wright began his career by establishing a home-based publishing company.

the type. By this time Orville had his own shop. Ed Sines recalled how it mystified a pressman for a Chicago printing house:

> One day he walked into the front office and asked if "that Wright press is running today." When we told him it was running at that time he said he would like to see it. Well, he went back into the pressroom, stood by the machine, looked at it, then sat down beside it and finally crawled underneath it. After he had been under the machine some little time he got up and said, "Well, it works, but I certainly don't see how it does the work.[14]

In his senior year Orville dropped out of school to concentrate on his printing business. With his new homemade press, he could now bid on church and business jobs and was planning to publish a weekly newspaper. He was confident these ventures would earn enough money to justify his quitting school.

Orville started putting together a press bigger than any he had ever built. He was not even sure what he would do with it—he just wanted the fun of building it.

This press was made out of scrap metal, wood, and the folding top of an old carriage. Its construction was so difficult that Orville had to ask his older brother for help. The suggestions Wilbur made were so odd that they seemed to violate the rules of mechanics. He figured out a way to use an old folding buggy top to place just the right amount of pressure on

WILBUR'S DARK DAYS

While Orville pursued his ambitions with typical enthusiasm, Wilbur's life seemed headed in the opposite direction. He had planned on entering Yale Divinity School and becoming a minister after high school—until a piece of wood turned his world upside down. It happened on a frozen lake during the winter of 1885–1886. During a hockey-like game called "shinny," someone swung a wooden club wildly and accidentally hit Wilbur in the mouth, knocking out most of his

A WORLD OF HIS OWN

Fred Howard, author of Wilbur and Orville: A Biography of the Wright Brothers *took stock of the brothers' differences and similarities as young men.*

"In many ways they were remarkably alike. Neither drank. Neither used tobacco, although Orville had tried it in his teens. Wilbur weighed around a hundred forty pounds and stood five feet ten. Orville was an inch or two shorter and a few pounds heavier. Their voices were similar—high-pitched and hard to tell apart if the listener was in an adjoining room.

Both had gray-blue eyes, but there was little facial resemblance. Orville had undistinguished features, more difficult to recall when he was clean-shaven than after he had grown a mustache. He had thick, curly dark brown hair. Wilbur had prominent ears, a cleft chin, and an open, firm face, stronger for the loss of his thin brown hair, which had all but disappeared by 1894. There were pronounced lines from the wings of his nostrils to the corners of his wide, expressive mouth. Wilbur was hard to rattle. Orville was more excitable, a constant talker at home or among friends. Compared to Wilbur he was a dandy, always well groomed even in the bicycle shop, where he wore sleeve cuffs and an apron of blue-and-white ticking to protect his clothing. He had always been the playful one, the prankster who dropped red pepper down the heat register in school. . . . Wilbur was more withdrawn. 'The strongest impression one gets of Wilbur Wright is of a man who lives largely in a world of his own," wrote a former schoolmate in describing a Fourth of July picnic at which Wilbur put up the swings for the children and then stood aloof from the crowd for much of the day."

The Wright brother's childhood home on Hawthorne Street in Dayton, Ohio.

upper teeth and leaving his face and lips a bloody mess.

The pain stayed with Wilbur for months, growing worse every time his mouth was worked on to fit it for false teeth. The injury was bad enough, but then doctors announced that his heart had been weakened by his reaction to the accident, causing nervous palpitations. They prescribed bed rest. To make matters worse, Wilbur developed a stomach disorder that would not go away.

People often died young in those days, and Wilbur worried that his life was nearly over. He had dreamed of going to Yale, but that dream now seemed dead. If his heart really were about to fail, then money spent to send him to college would be money wasted. He began to think of himself as an invalid who would never be able to return to an active life. The thought plunged him into a deep depression that lasted close to four years.

At first Wilbur did little but stay in his room and read. Besides dipping into the *Encyclopaedia Brittanica* and *Chambers's Cyclopaedia*, he read serious books like James Boswell's *Life of Johnson*, Edward Gibbon's *The Decline and Fall of the Roman Empire*, and histories of England and France. Then his mother's health began failing. After 1887 she was rarely able to get out of bed on her own. At the time, all of Wilbur's brothers and sisters were either at school or work during the day or had moved away. With Milton off on church business, Wilbur was often home alone with his mother.

A Son's Love

Every morning he carried her downstairs to the parlor, and every night he carried her back upstairs to bed. His father, describing the bond that formed between them, said, "He devoted himself to taking all care of her, and watching and serving her with a faithfulness and tenderness that cannot but shed happiness on him in life, and comfort him in his last moments. Such devotion of a son has rarely been equaled."[15]

Milton was convinced Wilbur's care added at least two years to Susan Wright's life. Still, Wilbur's lack of initiative worried the rest of the family. It seemed a shame that a young man with so much potential could not muster enough energy to leave the house. In a letter to Katharine, Reuchlin wrote, "What does Will do? He ought to do something. Is he still cook and chambermaid?"[16]

When Susan Wright died on July 4, 1889, Wilbur was twenty-two. Although the years he might have spent in college were already behind him, his depression was finally lifting and he was feeling healthier. Just as important, he had entered into a partnership with Orville—a partnership that, before long, would astound the world.

2 The Bicycle Builders

After Susan Wright's death in 1889 Wilbur and Orville, continued living at home with their sister, Katharine, for the next twenty-three years. That arrangement suited Milton Wright. He enjoyed having his children around when he returned from church business.

Continuing to live at home also relieved most of the financial pressure on Wilbur and Orville to go out and find a job with someone else. Also, since neither brother ever married, they also had far more free time than men with jobs and families, which gave them ample opportunity to pursue their interests.

Orville and Wilbur became successful businessmen. When problems arose, they solved them on their own, rarely asking outsiders for help. Their self-sufficiency proved invaluable when they later tack-

Orville, Katharine, and Wilbur Wright (left to right) lived with their widowed father well into adulthood.

led the problem of flight—an area where no one seemed to have definite answers.

Fascinated by the printing business, Orville began publishing a four-page weekly newspaper called the *West Side News* in the spring of 1889. He was so certain of his future as a printer that he did not return to high school for his senior year. Meanwhile Wilbur, who enjoyed writing and finally felt well enough to leave the house, was listed as the newspaper's editor.

The *West Side News* ended publication after a year when the brothers began publishing a daily newspaper instead. The *Evening Item* did a good job covering local news, and Wilbur often used his imagination to write eye-catching headlines in the style of the day. A story about a killer fire in Montreal was titled "Roasted in Red, Roaring and Terrible Flames," and "Death Locked in the Juice of a Poisonous Root"[17] reported the sad story of a French Canadian family who had died from eating bad parsnips.

The *Item* expired in August of 1890, a victim of fierce competition. There were twelve newspapers in Dayton that year and the bigger ones had the advantage of expensive high-speed presses. Wilbur and Orville went back to printing jobs for their regular customers. A few months later they tried to help out Paul Lawrence Dunbar, one of Orville's old classmates.

The son of a former slave, Dunbar would one day become a famous poet. He had written poetry for the *West Side News* and in December 1890, with the help of Wilbur and Orville, tried to put together a newspaper for Dayton's black commu-

In 1890, the Wright Brothers helped future poet Paul Lawrence Dunbar (pictured) establish a black community newspaper.

nity. Although that paper did not last long either, a little poem that Dunbar scratched on the wall of the print shop shows the high regard he had for his friend:

> Orville Wright is out of sight
> In the printing business.
> No other mind is half as bright
> As his'n is.[18]

WILBUR SUES HIS BROTHER

Like most brothers, Orville and Wilbur had disagreements. Used to being his own boss, Orville had to adjust when his older brother came to work with him.

Orville Wright (right) and a neighbor working on frames in Wright's bicycle shop.

One day, after some confusion over who was supposed to work on a particular job, Orville had harsh words for Wilbur. Although Wilbur thought Orville's actions were uncalled for, he did not lash back at his brother.

Instead, he drew up a phony legal document in which he pretended to sue Orville. In it he asked that an imaginary court make Orville apologize for his insulting conduct and requested that Orville "keep his mouth shut in future, lest he should again be guilty of befouling the spotless and innocent character of others."[19]

Wilbur and Orville each had a great sense of humor. Over the years, they learned to use them to ease tensions that might otherwise occur as they worked so closely together. That was not to say that they did not argue. In fact, they argued often. But they actually enjoyed most of their arguments.

"I love to scrap [argue] with Orv," Wilbur once announced. "Orv is such a good scrapper."[20] For the two of them, arguing was a way of tossing ideas back and forth until a solution was reached. There was nothing personal about it— sometimes they would even switch sides in the middle of an argument.

By the fall of 1892 any serious disagreements they might have had were forgotten as they began planning an exciting new venture: opening their own bicycle shop. Bicycling had become a national craze and the introduction of the safety bicycle (a bicycle with wheels of equal size) meant that bicycles could be ridden by just about anyone, even young women. As young men of their time, Wilbur and Orville participated in the craze. They took long rides in the country and Orville raced competitively, even winning several races.

The brothers were great mechanics and, after friends asked for help in fixing their bikes, Wilbur and Orville decided to open a shop to sell and repair bicycles. This business would be in addition to their print shop. The Wright Cycle Exchange opened in the spring of 1893 and business was very good that first year.

The shop took trade-ins, even though few people wanted to buy the old used high-wheel bikes. With typical ingenuity, Wilbur and Orville found a use for those four-foot-high wheels. They constructed a gigantic bicycle-built-for-two and then rode it through the streets of Dayton promoting their business.

The brothers were now a team, and the bike business provided them with great training in mechanics. Unfortunately, in northern cities like Dayton the bicycle businesses did not do well in the winter months, and Wilbur considered going back to college. In a letter to his father in the fall of 1894 he said, "I do not think that I am specially fitted for success in any commercial pursuit. . . . I have always thought I would like to be a teacher."[21]

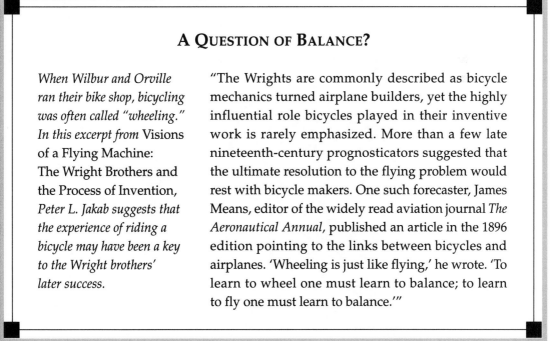

A QUESTION OF BALANCE?

When Wilbur and Orville ran their bike shop, bicycling was often called "wheeling." In this excerpt from Visions of a Flying Machine: The Wright Brothers and the Process of Invention, *Peter L. Jakab suggests that the experience of riding a bicycle may have been a key to the Wright brothers' later success.*

"The Wrights are commonly described as bicycle mechanics turned airplane builders, yet the highly influential role bicycles played in their inventive work is rarely emphasized. More than a few late nineteenth-century prognosticators suggested that the ultimate resolution to the flying problem would rest with bicycle makers. One such forecaster, James Means, editor of the widely read aviation journal *The Aeronautical Annual*, published an article in the 1896 edition pointing to the links between bicycles and airplanes. 'Wheeling is just like flying,' he wrote. 'To learn to wheel one must learn to balance; to learn to fly one must learn to balance.'"

Although his father agreed and offered to help pay for college, Wilbur did not follow up on the offer. Instead, he joined Orville in a second business venture. Hoping to expand their business beyond their immediate neighborhood, they opened a second bicycle shop in downtown Dayton. But the bicycle fad was fading by then and the new shop did not last beyond the fall of 1895.

A DO-IT-YOURSELF BUSINESS

By then the brothers were excited about a new challenge. After repairing bicycles for three years, they were sure they could build and design bicycles that were just as good or better than the brands they had been selling. As Orville put it in a letter to his father, "Our bicycle business is beginning to be a little slack, though we sell a wheel now and then. Repairing is pretty good. We expect to build our own wheels for next year. I think it will pay us, and give us employment during the winter."[22]

Orville loved solving mechanical problems, and turning their shop into a miniature bike factory allowed both brothers the opportunity to use their creativity. Together they built their own engine to

The brother's cycle shop doubled as a laboratory where ideas for their first flying machines took shape.

A TWENTY-TWO-POUND BEAUTY

In the April 17, 1896, issue of Snap-Shots of Current Events, *a weekly newspaper publication for Dayton cyclists, Wilbur and Orville proudly announced their new line of bicycles. Their ad was reprinted in Tom Crouch's* The Bishop's Boys.

"For a number of months, the Wright Cycle Co. has been making preparations to manufacture bicycles. After more delay than we expected, we are at last ready to announce that we will have several samples out in a week or ten days and will be ready to fill orders before the middle of the month. The Wright Special will contain nothing but high grade materials throughout, although we shall put it on the market at the exceedingly low price of $60. It will have large tubing, high frame, tool steel bearings, needle wire spokes, narrow tread and every feature of an up-to-date bicycle. Its weight will be about 22 pounds. We are very certain that no wheel on the market will run easier or wear longer than this one, and we will guarantee it in the most unqualified manner."

supply power to run the machinery, designed an electrical welding machine to build bike frames, and came up with other innovations.

In April 1896 they began selling their own bicycles. Each was hand-built to order and, because of the brothers' reputation for quality work, demand was high. During the next four years they sold some three hundred bicycles. Although they were not rich, they had become successful businessmen.

Their success was due in large part to their sister Katharine. She kept the household running smoothly while her two bachelor brothers concentrated on their work and whatever else interested them.

Orville and Wilbur were blessed with most of the benefits of an active family life but few of the time-consuming responsibilities. Since their older brother, Lorin, lived only a block away, his four children spent plenty of time with Uncle Wilbur and Uncle Orville.

Wilbur and Orville were the kind of uncles that kids love. Extremely patient with their nieces and nephews, they enjoyed playing games and making candy. If toys broke they not only fixed them, they often made them better than the originals.

"Grandpa Wright's house was a favorite place," remembered their niece, Leontine. "Sometimes there was picture taking, fascinating candy making, good reading sessions, and good games indoors and out." Leontine's sister, Ivonette, fondly recalled what happened when her mother ran errands downtown. "We were dropped off at the bicycle shop, and either Orville or Wilbur, or both, baby-sat us. They were never too busy to entertain us."[23]

Orville, a lifelong practical joker, rarely missed an opportunity to tease his nieces and nephews. One time, at Thanksgiving, he served up the turkey. His nieces and nephews preferred dark meat and were amazed that there seemed to be an endless supply. When someone remarked how good the turkey was, yet it tasted a little like duck, Orville could keep a straight face no longer. Grinning, he turned the platter around to show everyone that the turkey was only a front. Behind it was the duck that provided all the dark meat.

The practical jokes nearly ended in 1896, when Orville was twenty-five. In August of that year he came down with typhoid fever, an often fatal disease. For weeks he lay in bed near death and barely conscious, his temperature fluctuating between 103 and 105 degrees. Katharine and Wilbur took turns sitting by his bed, feeding him, and using sponges to keep him cool.

A NEW INTEREST

Finally, in early October the fever broke, and Orville began regaining strength. Right about that time the brothers became seriously interested in the problem

The death of aeronautics engineer Otto Lilienthal (pictured) reinvigorated the Wright brothers' interest in flying.

of flight. Two years earlier they had seen an article called "The Flying Man" in a popular magazine called *McClure's*. The article was accompanied by a series of striking photographs showing a German man named Otto Lilienthal soaring thirty feet above the ground on what today would be called a hang glider.

Lilienthal was a scientist who had devoted more than twenty years of his life to the study of flight. Since he had made thousands of glider flights, he undoubtedly knew more about the practical side of flying than anyone alive. He even built a cone-shaped hill so that he could always launch his glider into the wind.

Lilienthal's comments about the thrill of flying intrigued Wilbur and Orville. He once commented on the joys of soaring "over ravines and crowds of people who looked up in wonder."[24] But then, in August of 1896, the same month that Orville became sick, Wilbur was shocked by news out of Germany. While some fifty feet above the ground, Lilienthal's glider had caught a sudden gust of wind, turned sideways, and crashed to the ground. Lilienthal's back was broken and he died the next day.

The report made a big impression on Wilbur. "My own active interest in aeronautical problems dates back to the death of Lilienthal in 1896," he recalled years later. "The brief notice of his death which

---

NO HELP NECESSARY

In her Flight into History: The Wright Brothers and the Air Age, *Elsbeth Freudenthal noted how the Wright brothers' background uniquely prepared them to become inventors.*

"Most important was the fact that from the beginning they worked independently. The evidence available indicates that [as adults] neither Wilbur nor Orville ever worked for any other person, and that they never had the experiences of applying for or holding a job. Working for and by themselves, they developed the characteristics often shown by independent workers—the ability to plan a project and to carry it out. Used to being independent of others' opinions, ways of working, and standards, they had only their own standards to meet. Since they were serious young men, they set these standards high. The resulting qualities—determination to work alone and unaided by others and resoluteness in carrying out their own plans—were later to be responsible for their success, as well as for the personal dislike they sometimes aroused. The brothers were psychologically equipped to work independently of others' help, and were able to furnish for themselves the inner drive that independent workers must generate if they are to achieve their self-appointed goals."

appeared in the telegraphic news at that time aroused a passive interest which had existed from my childhood."[25]

There were other aeronautical developments that summer. Professor Langley of the Smithsonian flew two small, steam-powered model airplanes over the Potomac River near Washington, D.C. Meanwhile, on the sand dunes beside Lake Michigan, a railroad- and bridge-building engineer named Octave Chanute conducted his own gliding experiments. The longest of his flights lasted only 7.9 seconds, but the fact that experiments were now being done on this side of the Atlantic stirred new interest in flying.

When Orville was well enough to sit up in bed, he and Wilbur discussed Lilienthal's death. They wondered what had really happened to cause a man with so much experience to crash. Still, if they had any interest in picking up where he had left off, they kept it to themselves. After Orville was fully recovered, he returned to the shop and their new bike-building business.

BIRDS AND BOOKS

But their curiosity about aeronautics did not die. Over the next two years they read

Engineer Octave Chanute, designer of the flying machine shown right, spurred the brother's dream of flight.

WILBUR'S HAT TRICK

Carrie Kayler began working in the Wright household at age fourteen, staying on as a housekeeper until after Orville died in 1948. When biographer Fred C. Kelly was putting Miracle at Kitty Hawk: The Letters of Wilbur and Orville Wright *together in 1951, he talked with her about the differences between the two brothers and a sheepish grin that she remembered from half a century before.*

"Mr. Will was always more methodical than Mr. Orville, Carrie felt sure. When he came home from the bicycle shop at noon and for supper he would *always* do these things and in this order: come through the back door into the kitchen and drop his hat on the nearest chair; reach to the top of the cupboard where he kept a comb and carefully smooth down his fringe of hair; and then cross to the sink to wash his hands. After that he would go directly to a cracker box on the dining room sideboard, pick out one cracker and nibble it as he went to the front of the house. That was a signal to set food on the table.

Promptly, when the noon hour was over, Mr. Will would come through the kitchen, looking straight ahead and saying nothing. He'd go out the back door and down the alley. But in a minute he'd come back, with a queer little one-sided smile, for his hat. Mr. Orville, on the other hand, never once forgot his hat; and no matter how absorbed he was in what he was doing or thinking, he always knew what was going on around him."

everything they could on the subject at the Dayton library. Wilbur often spent his Sundays at a spot outside Dayton called the Pinnacles. There he would lie on his back with a pair of field glasses, studying the birds soaring effortlessly overhead.

Early in the spring of 1899 they came across a book on ornithology (the science and study of birds). It made them rethink the problem. As Orville would explain later, "We could not understand there was

anything about a bird that could not be built on a larger scale and used by man. If the bird's wings would sustain it in the air without the use of any muscular effort, we did not see why man could not be sustained by the same means."[26]

Even though their printing and bicycle businesses were doing well, Wilbur was not happy. He had a sense that they were capable of much more. "I entirely agree that the boys of the Wright family are all lacking in determination and push," he said. "None of us has as yet made particular use of the talent in which he excels other men, that is why our success has been very moderate."[27]

Wilbur was searching for a great problem to solve—a challenge worthy of his talents. In May of 1899, after a typically thorough study, he believed he had found one. The mystery of flight fascinated him and it seemed to be one of the few areas of study where someone without special training might make a contribution. Wilbur and Orville had time, talent, and interest—all they needed was knowledge. But as the two bicycle builders soon discovered, science knew surprisingly little about flight.

3 An Idea Takes Wing

By the summer of 1899 the Wright brothers had committed themselves to a serious study of all that science knew about flight. Once they completed their research they decided to experiment with some of their own ideas. Those experiments would eventually lead them to one of the most isolated places in America, Kitty Hawk, North Carolina. There they tested their theories in almost complete privacy.

At first Wilbur and Orville were humbled by what they found out about flight in the scientific literature. Some of the best minds in history had considered the problem and given it up as hopeless.

TACKLING THE IMPOSSIBLE

Many years after the Wright brothers flew, while testifying in a lawsuit, Wilbur described the psychological barrier he and Orville faced at the end of the nineteenth century. His remarks were reprinted in Tom Crouch's The Bishop's Boys.

"My brother and I became seriously interested in the problem of human flight in 1899. . . . We knew that men had by common consent adopted human flight as the standard of impossibility. When a man said, 'It can't be done; a man might as well try to fly,' he was understood as expressing the final limit of impossibility. Our own growing belief that man might nevertheless learn to fly was based on the idea that while thousands of the most dissimilar body structures, such as insects, fish, reptiles, birds and mammals, were flying every day at pleasure, it was reasonable to suppose that man might also fly. . . . We accordingly decided to write to the Smithsonian Institution and inquire for the best books relating to the subject."

These included the great inventor, Thomas Edison. They wondered whether they really could expect to do any better.

A few so-called flying machines had already been built by others. But none of them had really flown. The few that had left the ground had immediately crashed or fallen apart in the air. As Wilbur dryly put it, those machines were "guilty of almost everything except flying."[28]

Still, he and Orville were confident enough in their abilities to be excited by the challenge. Here was a field that was truly wide open. No one, for example, had even tried to design a system for controlling a machine once it had attained flight. To the kite-flying Wrights that seemed like a huge oversight. After all, glider pilots like Lilienthal had died precisely because they had lost control of their machines in the air.

On May 30, 1899, Wilbur wrote a letter to the Smithsonian Institution asking for information about flight. "I am about to begin a systematic study of the subject in preparation for practical work to which I expect to devote what time I can spare from my regular business. I wish to obtain such papers as the Smithsonian Institution has published on this subject, and if possible a list of other works in print in the English language."

Afraid he might be mistaken for a "barnyard engineer" (a term people used for inventors who did not approach a problem scientifically), Wilbur was careful to add, "I am an enthusiast but not a crank in the sense that I have some pet theories as to the proper construction of a flying machine."[29]

Within a week the Smithsonian responded with a list of books and four free pamphlets. The books included writings by Professor Samuel Langley of the Smithsonian and Octave Chanute. Chanute's *Progress in Flying Machines* was an invaluable resource. Published in 1894, it detailed all that was known about flight up until that time. Wilbur ordered all the books on the Smithsonian's list and read them over the summer. His research only increased the feeling that his pet theories might have something to offer.

THE WRONG APPROACH?

He and Orville concluded that most previous investigators had been going at the

The machine gun Hiram Maxim invented worked much better than his steam-propelled flying machine.

SCIENCE? WHAT SCIENCE?

Wilbur Wright was not impressed by what he saw when he began a serious study of the problem of flight in the summer of 1899. In One Day at Kitty Hawk: The Untold Story of the Wright Brothers and the Airplane *John Evangelist Walsh quotes Wilbur on what he found.*

"At that time there was no flying art in the proper sense of the word, but only a flying problem. Thousands of men had thought about flying machines, and a few had even built machines which they called flying machines, but these machines were guilty of almost everything except flying. Thousands of pages had been written on the so-called science of flying, but for the most part the ideas set forth, like the designs for machines, were mere speculation and probably ninety percent were false. Consequently, those who tried to study the science of aerodynamics knew not what to believe and what not to believe. Things which seemed reasonable were very often found to be untrue, and things which seemed unreasonable were sometimes true."

problem from the wrong angle. They had been so intent on getting a machine into the air, they had given little thought to what would happen once they got it there. That was certainly the case with inventor Hiram Maxim.

A brilliant engineer probably best known for his invention of the machine gun, Maxim built a huge flying machine —it weighed nearly four tons—in 1894. Powered by two steam engines, it consisted of a wooden platform with room for a pilot and three passengers, a water tank, a generator, and a "steering cabinet." This strange-looking apparatus had its first real test in England in August of 1894.

It was designed to run on rails with another set of guardrails a few inches above to prevent the whole machine from soaring away once it lifted off. That was a good idea since there was no way to control it in the air. After reaching a speed of forty-two miles per hour, Maxim's creation actually rose a few inches off the track. But then a section of guardrail broke off and became tangled with one of the propellers. Although he would state that "Propulsion and lifting are solved problems,"[30] that was not really true. Maxim's monster never "flew" again.

Maxim may have spent as much as one hundred thousand dollars building

Otto Lilienthal's engineless glider provided the Wright brothers with a crude model for their first flying machine.

his machine. In France, Clement Ader also spent at least that much money designing his own steam-powered contraptions. Despite claims that he had flown almost one thousand feet, actual records indicate his craft never did much more than lift off the ground for a few seconds. In 1897 the government cut off all funds for his project.

The Wright brothers would have agreed with the decision. They could not see the logic of building costly machines that would have crashed immediately had they ever gotten airborne. To them, it made more sense to learn *how* to fly first. That was one reason they were great admirers of German engineer, Otto Lilienthal.

Unlike Maxim, Lilienthal knew what it was like to fly. He had taken more than two thousand glider flights between 1891 and 1896. Like modern hang gliders, Lilienthal's gliders had no engines. The pilot simply jumped from a high place, usually into the wind. Without a doubt, Lilienthal had more practical experience than anyone in the world. And, although it was crude, he had devised a way to control his craft in the air. Lilienthal flew with his legs dangling down and balanced by shifting his weight forward or backward or from side to side.

A big problem, though, was that he was always reacting to his glider's movements rather than guiding them. Worse, if he did not react quickly enough when a powerful wind gust unbalanced his glider, he lost forward momentum and crashed. That seems to have been what happened the day he suffered his fatal injury.

The Wrights felt that they could come up with a safer, more efficient way to control a glider in flight. Just as in riding a bicycle, balance was crucial. Without it, a crash was certain. Or, as Wilbur put it, "the problem of equilibrium constituted the problem of flight itself."[31]

BIRDS PROVIDED A CLUE

Wilbur had reached the conclusion that balance was the key to flight after closely watching turkey vultures and other soaring birds. When a bird was rocked sideways by a gust of wind he noticed that it righted itself by twisting the tips of its wings in opposite directions. The leading edge of one wing would twist upward while the opposite wing would twist downward. As Wilbur put it, balance was attained by "utilizing dynamic reactions of the air instead of shifting weight."[32] He reasoned that if the wings of an aircraft could be made to do the same thing, a pilot could fly under any conditions.

However, making wing light enough to be bent—or warped, as they called it—yet strong enough to lift an aircraft would be difficult. While working late one night at the bicycle shop that summer, Wilbur stumbled upon a solution. A customer

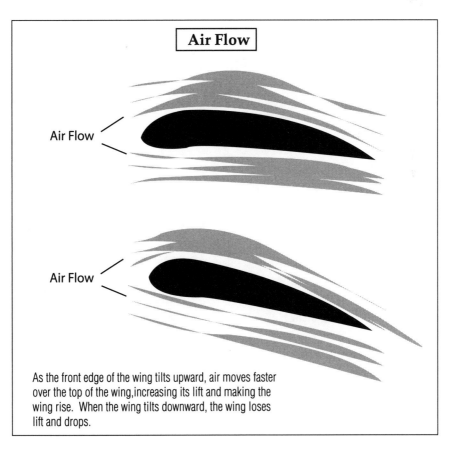

Air Flow

Air Flow

Air Flow

As the front edge of the wing tilts upward, air moves faster over the top of the wing, increasing its lift and making the wing rise. When the wing tilts downward, the wing loses lift and drops.

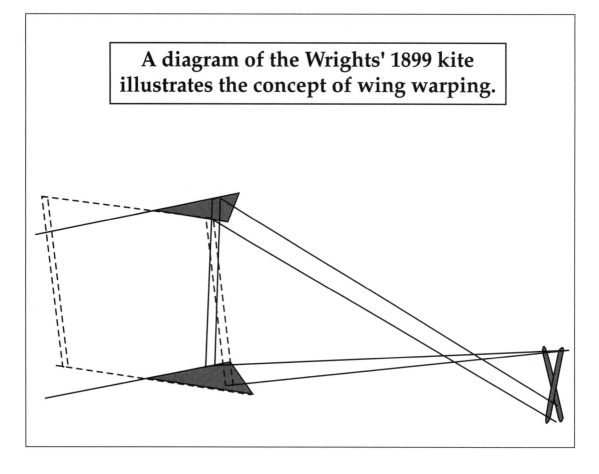

A diagram of the Wrights' 1899 kite illustrates the concept of wing warping.

came in and asked for a replacement inner tube for his bicycle. After removing a new one from the long narrow box it came in, Wilbur held the box in his hands. While talking with the customer he absentmindedly began twisting the ends in opposite directions. Suddenly, he realized that it might be possible to twist the cloth-covered wings of a flying machine in much the same way.

When he got home that night Wilbur talked the idea over with Orville. His brother was as enthusiastic about it as he was. Within a day or two they had built a small model of how such a machine might

look. After studying it for a few days, Wilbur began work on a biplane kite with a five-foot wingspan. Cords were attached to the tips of the wings so that he could try out the wing-warping mechanism.

Orville was away on a camping trip in late July when Wilbur tested the kite. The sight of a grown man flying such a huge kite was bound to attract attention. Wilbur preferred to test his ideas without an audience. If they did not work, at least people would not be laughing at him. He went to a field outside Dayton where the only witnesses were several curious boys. Although it took him a while to get the hang of it, Wilbur was delighted to find that the wing-warping system really worked. It was an exciting moment. He believed, correctly as it turned out, that he had solved one of the great problems of flight.

A week later Wilbur visited Orville's camp and excitedly told him what had happened. The brothers agreed that it was time to test wing warping on an even larger scale. "After a little time," Orville recalled, "we decided to experiment with a man-carrying machine embodying the principles of lateral control used in the kite model already flown." [33]

SEARCHING FOR THE PERFECT PLACE

They planned to fly the glider as a kite at first so that they could fully understand how the controls worked *before* risking their lives in the air. Construction of that first man-carrying glider took most of the winter. In the meantime, their calculations showed that a steady breeze of fifteen to sixteen miles per hour would be required to keep it aloft. Winds that strong were rare around Dayton, so Wilbur wrote to the Weather Bureau in Washington. They responded with a helpful list of wind velocities at 120 weather bureau stations around the United States.

Besides high winds, the ideal spot would offer privacy and soft sand for crash landings. While still trying to make a decision, Wilbur decided to seek advice from the country's greatest aeronautical expert. On May 13, 1900, he carefully composed a letter to Octave Chanute. Wilbur introduced himself with dry humor and typical humility:

> For some years I have been afflicted with the belief that flight is possible to man. My disease has increased in severity and I feel that it will soon cost me an increased amount of money if not my life. I have been trying to arrange my affairs in such a way that I can devote my entire time for a few months to experiment in this field. [34]

After discussing some of the reasons he believed Lilienthal failed, Wilbur outlined his plans to fly his glider as a kite in order to get more practical experience than any

Wilbur Wright solicited guidance and encouragement from esteemed engineer Octave Chanute (pictured).

other flyer ever had. At the end of his letter he asked for suggestions from Chanute:

> My business requires that my experimental work be confined to the months between September and January and I would be particularly thankful for advice as to a suitable locality where I could depend on winds of about fifteen miles per hour without rain or too inclement weather.[35]

Even though Chanute was one of the most distinguished engineers in America and Wilbur Wright was virtually unknown, Chanute was impressed by Wilbur's thoughts and wrote back immediately. He suggested beaches in California or Florida where sea breezes blew regularly. Al-

though Wilbur considered the scientist's suggestions, in the end he chose a place a little closer that neither he nor Orville had ever heard of before—Kitty Hawk, North Carolina.

Kitty Hawk was part of a two hundred-mile strip of sand beaches on North Carolina's Outer Banks. In 1900 it was one of the most isolated places in America, reachable only by boat. On August 3 Wilbur wrote a letter to the weather bureau station at Kitty Hawk concerning his plans. A week later Joseph Dosher, the telegraph operator, wrote back. "The beach here," he said, "is about one mile wide, clear of trees or high hills and extends for nearly sixty miles in the same condition."[36]

Captain William Tate and his wife in front of the Kitty Hawk Post Office.

A "Glider Resort"

After Wilbur wrote to the weather station at Kitty Hawk asking for a description of the beach, his letter was passed on to William Tate. Considered the most educated man in the community, his response to Wilbur convinced him that he had found the place for his experiments. His letter to Wilbur was reprinted in Peter L. Jakab and Rick Young's The Published Writings of Wilbur and Orville Wright.

"In reply I wrote: 'At Kitty Hawk there is a strip of bald sand beach [Kill Devil Hills], free from trees, with practically nothing growing on it except an occasional bunch of buffalo grass. This strip of beach is about 1500 yards wide from ocean to bay, and extends many miles down the coast. The average elevation is from 8 to 20 feet above sea level, but at certain places drifting sand hills have been piled up by the wind until some of them have reached an elevation of 75 to 100 feet above the plain. The prevailing winds are from the northeast, and these hills are very steep on the southwest side, but not so steep on the northeast side. I would say that they average from 20 to 45 degrees on the south side.' I did not say a word about transportation facilities, neither did I give a word of direction about how to get to Kitty Hawk. Mr. Wright never forgot to joke me about this lack of information, which no doubt was impressed on him during the wearisome trip from Elizabeth City to Kitty Hawk. Wilbur Wright must have been thoroughly sold on Kitty Hawk as a glider resort. He never went to the trouble to write further, but made his preparations and left Dayton for Kitty Hawk."

Kill Devil Hills, near Kitty Hawk, North Carolina.

Dosher suggested Wilbur bring a tent since there was no place to rent a room. He also passed Wilbur's letter along to local businessman, William Tate. Tate sent a friendly invitation to Wilbur. "If you decide to try your machine here & come I will take pleasure in doing all I can for your convenience & success & pleasure, & I assure you you will find a hospitable people when you come among us."[37]

If Wilbur's mind was not made up by then, Tate's warm letter decided the issue. The rest of August was a blur of activity as he readied himself and his glider for the train trip to the East Coast. Most of the disassembled flying machine was packed in a large crate. Unfortunately, there was no way to pack the eighteen-foot spruce spars needed for the wings. Wilbur decided he would buy them just before he hired a boat to take him across Albemarle Sound to Kitty Hawk.

The Adventure Begins

On the evening of September 6, 1900, Wilbur boarded a train for the East Coast. A day later he arrived at a hotel in Norfolk, Virginia. The next morning, when he went looking for spruce to rebuild the plane's wings, he was dismayed to discover none was available. He had to settle for white pine, and the longest spars he could find were only sixteen feet.

Shorter wings meant that stronger winds would be needed to keep the glider aloft. Still, Wilbur had no other options.

Wilbur had planned on hiring someone in Elizabeth City to take him across Albemarle Sound to Kitty Hawk, a distance of roughly thirty-five miles. To his surprise, it took him three days before he found anyone who had even heard of Kitty Hawk.

A man named Israel Perry finally agreed to take Wilbur over to Kitty Hawk in his leaky schooner. After a harrowing journey (they ran into a dangerous storm), Wilbur finally arrived at Kitty Hawk on the night of September 12. If he had any doubts about the place's isolation, they must have ended on that trip. It had taken him longer to go the thirty-five miles to Kitty Hawk than it had to reach North Carolina from Dayton.

Two days after his arrival Wilbur began putting together his glider. He had to redesign many of the parts because of the shorter wings. The wing covers also had to be recut and resewn. Then, on September 28, Orville arrived. The two brothers set up camp in the sand a half mile from the nearest house, their tent securely roped to a tree so it would not blow away.

A week later the glider was ready. At last, after over a year of planning and preparation, they were about to find out whether all their work had paid off.

4 Flight School

Over two years, beginning in the fall of 1900, the Wright brothers would spend some eighteen weeks camping out near Kitty Hawk on North Carolina's Outer Banks. Despite danger, discomfort, and disappointment, these were among the happiest days of their lives. "There were hills there in plenty," Orville recalled later, "and not too many people about to scoff. Building that first glider was the best fun we'd ever had."[38]

While enjoying themselves thoroughly, the brothers undertook the most intensive flight testing ever attempted. In addition, they built three gliders, modifying each as the situation demanded. They were their own test pilots—as well as their own mechanics and aircraft designers. By the end of October 1902 they had mastered the principles of gliding flight and developed the basic system of flight control that aviators have used ever since.

In the fall of 1900, however, they had no clear idea where their experiments would lead. To avoid ridicule they had encouraged friends and acquaintances to think of their trip as a vacation in which they would spend some time on their flying "hobby."

Wilbur and Orville chose three large sand dunes just south of Kitty Hawk to practice their hobby. Residents called the area Kill Devil Hills, and the biggest sand dune was simply called Kill Devil Hill. John Daniels, a member of the Kill Devil Hills Lifesaving Station, recalled his reaction the first time he laid eyes on the Wrights. "When they first came down to Kill Devil Hills . . . and begun to experiment with their funny-looking kites we just thought they were a pair of crazy fools. We laughed about 'em, because they were as nice boys as you'd ever hope to see."[39]

Wilbur had not even told his father exactly what he was up to. Soon after arriving at Kitty Hawk he wrote to Milton, outlining his plans and reassuring him about the risks:

In my experiments I do not expect to rise many feet from the ground and in case I am upset there is nothing but soft sand to strike on. I do not intend to take dangerous chances, both because I have no wish to get hurt and because a fall would stop my experimenting, which I would not like at all. The man who wishes to keep at the problem long enough to really learn something positively must not take dangerous risks. Carelessness and overconfidence are

"A Pair of Poor Nuts"

In an interview reprinted in Peter L. Jakab and Rick Young's The Published Writings of Wilbur and Orville Wright, *John Daniels remembered watching the strange behavior of the Wright brothers from the Kill Devil Hills Lifesaving Station.*

"We couldn't help thinking they were just a pair of poor nuts. We'd watched them from the windows of our station. They'd stand on the beach for hours at a time just looking at the gulls flying, soaring, dipping. They seemed to be interested mostly in gannets. Gannets are big gulls with a wing spread of five or six feet. They would watch gannets for hours.

They would watch the gannets and imitated the movements of their wings with their arms and hands. They could imitate every movement of the wings of those gannets; we thought they were crazy, but we just had to admire the way they could move their arms this way and that and bend their elbows and wrist bones up and down and which-a-way, just like the gannets moved their wings.

But they were a long way from being fools. We began to see that when they got their glider working so that they could jump off into the air for several minutes, gradually gliding down to the beach almost as graceful as a gannet could have done it."

usually more dangerous than deliberately accepted risks.[40]

As it turned out, the risks that first year were minimal. Because of Wilbur's inability to find eighteen-foot spars, the glider was two feet shorter than planned. That meant that much stronger winds—around twenty-five miles an hour—were required to keep it in the air with a man aboard. Even at Kitty Hawk, winds that strong were infrequent.

Still, on the first windy day that they tested their glider, there was a moment of excitement. That morning they flew the glider as an unmanned kite. It took to the air so easily that Wilbur could not resist climbing aboard. With Orville and Bill Tate holding on to tether ropes, he rose perhaps fifteen feet into the air. Suddenly, as the craft began bobbing up and down he yelled, "Let me down!"

After he had safely reached the ground, Orville—always the more impulsive of

View of early Wright glider flown as a kite near Kitty Hawk.

the two—was a little upset. He could not understand why Wilbur had ended the experiment just when it was getting interesting. Wilbur's only explanation was, "I promised Pop I'd take care of myself."[41]

LEARNING FROM THE WIND

Wilbur's few moments in the air had convinced him that further unmanned testing was necessary. For most of their remaining time at Kitty Hawk that fall, they flew the glider as a kite, working the controls from the ground. Meanwhile, they took careful measurements of the wind speed and loaded up the glider with various weights of chain to see how it reacted under different conditions.

The wing-warping system worked well, but there were other problems to solve. When Wilbur could not get the elevator (the tail) to work as he wanted, Orville's perseverance and good humor came in handy. "We tried it with the tail in front, behind, and every other way," he wrote to Katharine. "When we got through, Will was so mixed up that he couldn't even theorize. It has been with considerable effort that I have succeeded in keeping him in the flying business at all."[42]

They eventually got the elevator working to their satisfaction—although it would become an even bigger problem the following year. Just before leaving for home in 1900, Wilbur wanted to try one more day of manned gliding. Since the wind was not strong enough at Kitty Hawk, he, Orville, and Bill Tate made the four-mile trip south to the sand dunes at Kill Devil Hills. Then Orville and Bill, each at a wing tip, ran downhill holding the glider level until they could not keep up any longer. It was hard work but the results were so good that they spent the whole day at it.

Wilbur had his best day of gliding ever. Some lasted as long as fifteen seconds. Those glides were also noteworthy in that Wilbur attempted something that other gliders had always considered suicidal. Instead of hanging from the wings he lay face down in a prone "belly buster" position, much like a child sledding down a hill. Originally he had planned on sit-

---

TIME TO GET OFF THE FENCE

This excerpt from Tom Crouch's The Bishop's Boys *was taken from a speech Wilbur made to some Chicago engineers in 1901. It describes his state of mind just before he began experimenting at Kitty Hawk.*

Wilbur Wright

"Now there are two ways of learning how to ride a fractious horse. One is to get on him and learn by actual practice how each motion and trick may be best met; the other is to sit on a fence and watch the beast a while, and then retire to the house and at leisure figure out the best way of overcoming his jumps and kicks. The latter system is the safest; but the former, on the whole, turns out the larger proportion of good riders. It is very much the same in learning to ride a flying machine; if you are looking for perfect safety, you will do well to sit on the fence and watch the birds; but if you really wish to learn, you must mount a machine and become acquainted with its tricks by actual trial."

CONTROL WAS KEY

In his book Wings of Feathers, Wings of Flame, *Norman Smith points out how, unlike virtually every other experimenter, the Wright brothers immediately zeroed in on the most critical aspect of learning how to fly.*

"In their study of the literature on aviation, the Wrights found that Lilienthal and other glider pilots had met disaster because they could not control their machines in the air. Gliders of this time were balanced by the pilot shifting his own weight. This method was clumsy and could not be relied upon, as several crashes had proved. The Wrights decided to find a better means of balancing a glider in flight.

Thus, even before they really began work on the problems of flight, the Wright brothers singled out the most important problem which had not yet been solved: how to *balance* and *control* the flying machine in the air. If a gust tipped the machine sideways, a control was needed to raise the low wing. If a machine dipped into a dive or a climb, another control was needed to return the machine to the desired altitude. The success of the Wright brothers in developing the first airplane is due largely to their great wisdom in selecting and solving this all-important problem of control."

ting up when the time came to land, but that did not prove necessary. Although he occasionally got a faceful of sand, the position greatly reduced wind resistance and proved no more dangerous than sitting upright.

As they packed up to head home for Dayton the next day, the brothers were proud of their progress. Their methods worked even better than they had hoped. For the first time ever, a glider in flight had been controlled by a system of wires and levers. That was a huge improvement over swinging one's weight back and forth in reaction to wind gusts the way Lilienthal had.

Wilbur and Orville spent the winter making plans for a new, improved glider. The design was much like their 1900 glider, although its wingspan of twenty-two feet made it the largest glider ever built. The brothers were so eager to try it out that they could hardly wait for fall, their bike shop's slow season.

Mosquito Bites and Disappointing Flights

On July 7, 1901, they left for the Carolina coast. A week earlier, Octave Chanute visited them in their Dayton home. Impressed by their progress, he arranged to visit them later that summer on the Outer Banks. He also arranged for two other visitors to Kitty Hawk: Edward Huffaker and George Spratt.

Huffaker was a Tennessee aeronautical experimenter with a master's degree in physics. He was working on a glider of his own. Spratt was a young doctor from Coatesville, Pennsylvania, who had always been fascinated with flying. In theory, because of the risk of crashes and the isolation of Kitty Hawk, it made sense to have a doctor around. In truth, Wilbur and Orville really did not want or need anyone to help them with their experiments. But they were too polite to say so to Chanute.

The brothers arrived at Kitty Hawk on July 11 and set up camp at Kill Devil Hills, near the place where Wilbur had flown the year before. It took them three days to build a hangar for the new glider. According to Orville, it was "a grand institution, with awnings at both ends."[43]

About a week later Huffaker arrived in camp, and so did a gigantic swarm of mosquitoes. "The agonies of typhoid fever with its attending starvation are as nothing in comparison," Orville wrote home. "The sand and grass and trees and hills and everything were crawling with them. They chewed us clean through our underwear and socks."[44]

Despite heat during the day and mosquitoes at night, the glider was fully assembled by July 26. The next day Wilbur

The Wrights' Kitty Hawk work shed was unusually crowded in August of 1901. From left to right: Octave Chanute, Orville Wright, Edward Huffaker, and Wilbur Wright (standing).

THE KITTY HAWK CURE

In Miracle at Kitty Hawk, *Fred C. Kelly recalls how Wilbur and Orville regarded their trips to North Carolina as welcome vacations. The sun, sea, fresh air, and exercise always seemed to do them good. And, as this August 20, 1902, letter from Katharine Wright to her father makes clear, everyone in the family was happy to see them go.*

"The flying machine is in process of making now. Will spins the sewing machine around by the hour while Orv squats around marking the places to sew. There is no place in the house to live but I'll be lonesome enough by this time next week and wish that I could have some of this racket around.

Will and Orv . . . really ought to get away for a while. Will is thin and nervous and so is Orv. They will be all right when they get down in the sand where the salt breezes blow, etc. They insist that if you aren't well enough to stay out on your trip you must come down with them. They think that life at Kitty Hawk cures all ills you know."

made seventeen glides. But from the very beginning there were unexpected problems. Disappointingly, the lift of the wings was only a third of what the Lilienthal tables had predicted. And the elevator worked poorly—Wilbur had to fight constantly to keep the glider's nose from pitching straight down or straight up.

Even worse, a problem they were sure had been solved was not solved at all. For some mysterious reason, when they made tighter turns using wing warping, the glider's wings sometimes moved in a direction opposite to the one intended. This sideslipping was, as Wilbur wrote to Chanute, "a very unlooked-for-result and one which completely upsets our theories as to the causes which produce the turning to right and left."[45]

Neither Huffaker or Chanute (who arrived in camp on August 5) realized how devastating these setbacks were. After witnessing glides of more than three hundred feet, Huffaker could not hide his enthusiasm. Chanute was equally impressed. "He is astonished at our mechanical facility," Wilbur noted, "and, as he attributes his own failures to the lack of this, he thinks the problem solved when these difficulties are overcome, while we expect to find further difficulties of a theoretical nature which must be met by new mechanical designs."[46]

Chanute was the first of many to overestimate the importance of the Wright brothers' mechanical aptitude. In years to come, the brothers would be dismissed as a couple of "bicycle repairmen" who had somehow gotten lucky. They were, of course, superb mechanics, but Wilbur, in particular, was constantly testing and refining theories of flight.

Yet if Lilienthal's tables were in error, then those theories had no firm scientific basis. Wilbur had a very low tolerance for uncertainty. Despite the praise of his distinguished visitors, he was near despair. The year had begun with high hopes that they could build a machine that would not only fly but be stable in flight. Now, after months of hard work, the goal seemed even further away than ever. Extremely disappointed, the brothers headed home in August, doubting they would ever resume their experiments:

> Although we had broken the record for distance in gliding, and although Mr. Chanute, who was present at that time, assured us that our results were

better than had ever before been attained, yet when we looked at the time and money which we had expended, and considered the progress made and the distance yet to go, we considered our experiments a failure.[47]

The brothers were on the verge of quitting. Orville recalled that on the train ride home, a depressed Wilbur had stated, "Not within a thousand years would man ever fly!"[48] It was Octave Chanute—along with a boost from Katharine Wright—who found a way to shake Wilbur's depression.

WILL GOES TO CHICAGO

On August 29 Chanute invited Wilbur to come to Chicago and speak before the Western Society of Engineers on his glid-

The Wright brothers' compiled the first accurate data on lift and drag using this wind tunnel.

ing experiments. Still in a down mood, Wilbur was not interested, but Katharine changed his mind. As she wrote in a letter to her father, "Will was about to refuse but I nagged him into going. He will get acquainted with some scientific men and it may do him a lot of good."[49]

It would be Wilbur's first public speech. Normally, women did not attend talks by the Western Society of Engineers, but interest for this talk was particularly high. That is why Chanute felt it necessary to ask Wilbur whether it would be all right if women were in the audience. Wilbur responded, "I will already be as badly scared as it is possible for a man to be, so that the presence of ladies will make little difference to me."[50] He need not have worried. With his knack for explaining complex ideas clearly, the lecture was a huge success.

After Wilbur returned from Chicago the two brothers set about building a body of aeronautical data they could trust. Working upstairs in their bicycle shop that winter, they discovered more about flying than anyone else had in the history of the world. And they did so while using amazingly simple materials—a fan, a wooden box, cut-up hacksaw blades, and small pieces of sheet metal shaped with tin shears.

With these simple items they built a wind tunnel in which they tested different wing shapes. They were not the first to build a wind tunnel, but they were the first to make accurate and precise measurements of lift and drag (resistance). A typical example of their genius is the homemade balance they made out of hacksaw blades and wire. It measured the lift of the tiny wings they fashioned from sheet metal.

Wilbur's depression was forgotten as the two brothers became totally caught up in the excitement of discovery. In two months they tested about two hundred different wing configurations. As Orville would recall, "Wilbur and I could hardly wait for morning to come to get at something that interested us. *That's* happiness!"[51]

THE THRILL OF DISCOVERY

Every single test took them further into unexplored territory. When they had finished, they felt both relief and renewed excitement. No longer did they have to risk their lives by relying on questionable figures provided by others. They had double-checked all the data themselves and were certain they knew how to make wings that would fly.

It was this knowledge they incorporated into the glider they built and then flew at Kill Devil Hills, beginning on September 19, 1902. The brothers were delighted with their initial tests—the new wings generated far greater lift than in previous years.

The 1902 glider featured other innovations. For the first time the warping mechanism was controlled by a hip cradle, a device that allowed the pilot to initiate turns by shifting his hips from side to side. In addition, the glider now had a double vertical tail. It was hoped that this would cut down on the mysterious side-slipping problem.

Dan Tate (left) and Wilbur Wright fly the second of the Wright gliders.

Wilbur made about twenty-five glides on September 19 and fifty the following day. On September 23, for the first time, Orville began learning how to fly the glider. He turned out to be a natural pilot, but after a morning of short glides, disaster struck. When one wing tilted sharply toward the ground, Orville shifted the hip cradle to regain control. But he forgot to pay attention to the elevator, and consequently the glider's nose rose skyward and the craft slipped sideways. Orville had

flown into a complete stall, the same condition that had killed Lilienthal and others.

He hung on with all his might as, almost in slow motion, the glider fell thirty feet and slammed hard into the dunes. As Wilbur and Dan Tate raced toward the wreck, they expected the worst. Yet, when they reached the severely damaged craft, they were amazed to find that Orville had not even suffered a scratch. It was a close call and a sobering reminder of the danger they put themselves in on every flight.

A few days later they had rebuilt the glider and were flying again. As long as they flew straight or banked gently, the craft behaved beautifully. But if they turned too sharply or the wind hit the glider just right, it would repeat the deadly sideslip that led to stalls, spins, and crashes. They were encountering what would one day be called "tailspin," which occurs when a plane banks sharply enough to cause the inside wing to lose the ability to lift. With only one wing providing lift, the plane starts spinning uncontrollably.

ORVILLE'S BRAINSTORM

Wilbur and Orville discussed the sideslipping problem constantly, debating solutions long into the night. They both felt that the tail was the source of the problem —although neither was sure why. Although they did not realize it at the time, they were wrestling with the last great problem of flight control. To fly safely, an aircraft must be controlled in three axes of movement: pitch, roll, and yaw.

Their elevator controlled pitch (nose pointing up or down) and wing warping controlled roll (rotating from side to side). But as yet they had no way to control yaw (the skidding movement that occurs when an aircraft turns sharply). It was Orville who hit upon an explanation and possible solution. After another late-night debate, he found himself unable to sleep. At breakfast next morning he excitedly told Wilbur his idea.

While one brother piloted the glider the other shared in the excitement from the ground.

The Wright brothers test their number three glider. Soon they would make the leap to engine-powered airplanes.

When the glider began to sideslip, wind currents sometimes hit the tail and added to the turning movement. In some cases, the entire craft would pivot about the tail. What if, he asked, they made the tail fin movable? That would allow the pilot to compensate for the pivoting tendency and keep the machine headed in the direction intended. To Orville's surprise, Wilbur liked the idea immediately, but he did not like the idea of another control to operate. Why not, he asked, link it directly with the wing-warping cradle so that the rudder would move automatically when the wings were warped?

They could hardly wait to begin work on the new tail rudder. It was mounted on a single tail fin and, once installed, worked beautifully. In the last weeks of the month they made over one thousand flights, several of them covering more than six hundred feet. In a letter to Katharine, Orville could barely contain his excitement:

In two days we made over 250 glides. . . . We have gained considerable proficiency in the handling of the machine now, so that we are able to take it out in any kind of weather. Day before yesterday we had a wind of 16 meters per second or about 30 miles per hour, and glided in it without any trouble. That was the highest wind a gliding machine was ever in, so that we now hold all the records! The largest machine that we handled in any kind [of weather], made the longest distance glide, the longest time in the air, the smallest angle of descent, and the highest wind!!! Well, I'll leave the rest of the "blow" till we get home.[52]

By the time they left Kill Devil Hills in late October, they were experienced pilots confident they could make the next step—design of an airplane that could take off and fly under its own power.

Chapter

5 The Whopper Flying Machine

After the Wright brothers returned to Dayton they assumed that building a powered flying machine would be a simple matter. All they needed to do was add an engine and propellers. In fact, those two additions proved to be among the most challenging engineering problems they ever faced.

While overcoming these technical hurdles Wilbur and Orville built the first airplane engine and invented the world's first operational airplane propeller. Then, after returning to the Outer Banks in the fall of 1903, they persevered through bad weather and equipment breakdowns to achieve success at almost the last possible moment.

The aircraft they built in 1903—they nicknamed it the *Flyer*—had a wingspan of forty feet. That was eight feet longer than the 1902 glider. At over six hundred pounds it was almost five hundred pounds

With the addition of an engine and propellers, the 1903 Wright Flyer *model biplane made the first of the brothers' powered flights.*

heavier than their previous glider. That was why they sometimes called it the "whopper flying machine."

Construction of the engine had begun in December 1902 in the Wright brothers' Dayton bicycle shop. Their calculations showed that it must weigh no more than two hundred pounds and produce at least eight to nine horsepower (a measurement of an engine's strength). Earlier, Wilbur wrote to manufacturers of gasoline engines asking about buying an engine of that size.

But no one sold an engine that light and no one was interested in building one either. With typical resourcefulness, the brothers decided they would build it themselves. Their mechanic, Charley Taylor, who had never built an engine before, was assigned the job, and Orville designed the engine.

"We didn't make any drawings," Taylor recalled later. "One of us would sketch out the part we were talking about on a piece of scratch paper and I'd tack the sketch over my bench."[53] Taylor finished the engine on February 12, 1903. It was crude and very noisy, but at twelve horsepower was even stronger than they hoped. Unfortunately, on its second day of testing the bearings froze and the crankcase shattered. That meant a new crankcase would have to be built. Although the project was set back several months, Taylor had the rebuilt engine working again by May.

THE PROPELLER PUZZLE

In the meantime, Orville and Wilbur were attacking their most difficult problem

Orville Wright (left), mechanic Charles Taylor (center), and automobile inventor Henry Ford look over historical drawings in the Wrights' engine shop.

ever—designing propellers to get their machine into the air. Typically, they would not just build some propellers and hope they would work. They did not have the time or money for that kind of guesswork. As always, they approached things scientifically, leaving nothing to chance.

It was crucial that they know beforehand exactly how much thrust their propellers would create. After all, a boat propeller, no matter how inefficient, could still move a boat forward a little. But if an airplane propeller could not provide the thrust needed to lift a plane into the air, it would be useless.

Propellers had been in use for almost a century on ships and boats. Wilbur and Orville felt certain there must be scientific data on how they worked. With such data it would be relatively simple to convert water pressure to air pressure and calculate how efficient an airplane propeller would be. But they were disheartened to discover that there was no data.

No one in the world had the slightest idea of how to measure the efficiency of any kind of propeller. As Orville described in a magazine article written years later, there was a reason for that— the problem was fiendishly difficult. "With the machine moving forward, the air flying backward, the propellers turning sidewise, and nothing standing still, it seemed impossible to find a starting point from which to trace the various simultaneous reactions."[54]

Many aeronautical experts think the work the Wright brothers did on propellers was some of the most extraordinary work they ever did. With only pencil and paper—they filled five notebooks with their calculations—they devised a mathematical formula to explain how a propeller worked. The formula worked so well that the thrust their propellers achieved were within 1 percent of their calculations. It was an astounding achievement.

"They Sure Got Awfully Hot"

It was not a peaceful process, either— there were arguments over nearly every detail. "The boys were working out a lot of theory in those days and occasionally they would get into terrific arguments," Taylor recalled. "They'd shout at each other something terrible. I don't think they ever really got mad, but they sure got awfully hot."[55]

Yet, no matter how heated the argument, Will and Orville retained the rare capacity to listen fully to the other person's point of view. "One morning, following the worst argument I ever heard," Taylor remembered, "Orv came in and said he guessed he'd been wrong and they ought to do it Wil's [sic] way." A few minutes later, Wil came in and said he'd been thinking it over and perhaps Orv was right."[56] Before long, the brothers were shouting at each other again—only now each had adopted the other's original position!

One of the brothers' more brilliant insights was to think of propeller blades as rotating wings. That meant they could use the wind tunnel results from 1902 to design propeller blades with maximum thrust. The blades they finally ended up

Wilbur Wright displays the revolutionary propeller design of the Wright Flyer II *biplane.*

with were revolutionary—they looked more like twisted wings than the screw-shaped propellers used to drive ships.

Besides propeller design, Wilbur and Orville had to figure out how long the blades should be, how wide, how much they should curve, and how fast they should rotate. When they finished their figuring, the results were almost exactly as predicted. With justifiable pride, Orville wrote to a friend that summer:

> During the time the engine was building we were engaged in some very heated discussions on the principles of screw propellers. We had been unable to find anything of value in any of the works to which we had access, so that we worked out a theory of our own on the subject, and soon discov-

ered, as we usually do, that all the propellers built heretofore are *all wrong*, and then built a pair of propellers 8-1/8 ft. in diameter, based on our theory, which are *all right!* (till we have a chance to test them down at Kitty Hawk and find out differently). Isn't it astonishing that all these secrets have been preserved for so many years just so that we could discover them![57]

PATENT PROBLEMS

While the brothers were busy constructing the *Flyer,* they found time to make their first application for a patent. After years of work, they wanted to be protected from someone stealing their hard-won discoveries. But the process turned out to be extremely frustrating. In March, the U.S. Patent Office denied the Wrights' application.

The patent examiner ruled that their machine was clearly "incapable of performing its intended function."[58] That must have been news to the Wright brothers. Wilbur wrote back, this time sending along a cardboard inner-tube box to help the examiner understand wing warping. That did not work either. The box was dismissed as "of no assistance" and the application denied again.

Wilbur and Orville were discovering that the U.S. Patent Office, just like the general public, had difficulty believing they had done what they said they had done. It would take three years before they received patent protection in the United States. In the meantime, they applied for patents in France, Germany, and Great Britain. But because the laws in Europe denied a patent if information about it had been published previously, the Wrights were not eager to reveal details of their control system.

In the years to come they would be accused of holding back American aviation because of their secrecy. But the brothers felt it was unfair for someone else to make money from their discoveries when they had done all the work.

Still, patent problems were the last thing on Wilbur and Orville's minds when they arrived at Kitty Hawk in late September 1903. Although confident their machine would be able to fly, they had no way of knowing for sure until they actually tried it. Since the *Flyer* had been shipped to Kitty Hawk in pieces, it took about a month to assemble.

A FINE START, THEN FRUSTRATION

The brothers arrived in camp on a Friday and started building a shed for the *Flyer*. On Monday, however, the weather was so good that they took most of the day off to practice with their 1902 glider. "We took the machine out and spent the finest day we have ever had in practice," Wilbur

The Wrights were relentless about practicing with their early glider.

The Aerodrome, *a powered airplane designed by Samuel Langley, was developed in this workshop.*

wrote to Octave Chanute. "We made about 75 glides, nearly all of more than 20 seconds' duration."[59]

One of their glides was more than thirty seconds, which beat all their former records. Every few days that fall, the brothers could not resist taking time off to practice their flying. Before long Orville would hold the world's record for a glider flight.

Although they were not aware of it at first, they had competition for a powered flying machine. On October 7, Samuel Langley's *Great Aerodrome* was launched on the Potomac River near Washington. A well-respected astronomer, Langley was also director of the Smithsonian Institution.

The government had given Langley a fifty thousand dollar grant to develop a flying machine capable of carrying a man.

By the fall of 1903 his *Aerodrome* was ready for its first flight test. The ungainly aircraft—the *Washington Post* called it "The Buzzard"[60]—was powered by a gasoline engine and propellers. Langley had come up with an elaborate scheme for launching his creation. Using a catapult, it would take off from the top of a houseboat anchored in the Potomac River near Washington, D.C.

On launch day, October 7, the pilot was an engineer named Charles Manley. Since the control mechanism had never been tested, Manley was along mostly for the ride. As it turned out, only his swimming skills were put to the test. After he revved up the engine, the *Aerodrome* moved along its launching rail and then dove straight into the river. Soaked but unhurt, Manley was fished out of the water.

A second trial on December 8 was, if anything, an even greater embarrassment. Before hundreds of spectators the craft sped down its sixty-foot track, flipped over on its back, and dropped like a stone into the icy water.

The newspapers were quick to ridicule the whole affair. "Langley's Dream Develops the Qualities of a Duck. It Breaks Completely in Two, but Without Even an Expiring Quack"[61] read one headline from the *Raleigh News and Observer*. The *Charlotte Observer* noted "As Bad as Darius Green, Langley Airship Total Wreck."[62]

Word of Langley's troubles soon reached the Outer Banks. "I see that Langley has had his fling, and failed," wrote Wilbur in another letter to Chanute. "It

"WE EXPECT NO TROUBLE FROM OUR BIG MACHINE"

After hearing of Langley's first failure, Orville confidently wrote to his sister Katharine on November 1, 1903. This excerpt is taken from Fred. C. Kelly's Miracle at Kitty Hawk.

"I suppose you have read in the papers the account of the failure of Langley's big machine. He started from a point 60 feet in the air and landed 300 feet away, which is a drop of 1 foot for every 5 forward. We are able, from this same height, to make from 400 to 600 feet without any motor at all, so that I think his surfaces must be very inefficient. They found they had no control of the machine whatever, though the wind blew but 5 miles an hour at the time of the test. That is the point where we have a great advantage. We have been in the air hundreds and hundreds of times, and have pretty well worked out the problem of control. We find it much more difficult to manage the machine when trying to soar in one spot than when traveling rapidly forward. We expect no trouble from our big machine at all in this respect. Of course we are going to thoroughly test the control of it on the hills before attaching the motor. We are highly pleased with our progress so far this year."

Samuel Langley, developer of the Aerodrome.

scrapped plans to test the biplane's control systems by first flying it as a glider. Instead, the very first flight would be as a powered airplane. It was a huge gamble since the flight characteristics of a powered plane would surely be different than those of a glider.

While the brothers waited for the return of the propeller shafts, they passed the time reading. Orville, always one to keep his mind busy, resumed teaching himself French and German. Finally, on November 20 the shafts arrived from Dayton. But again they faced agonizing frustration. While testing the engine they discovered a hairline crack in one of the propeller shafts. Had it gone unnoticed, it could have led to a disastrous crash.

seems to be our turn to throw now, and I wonder what our luck will be."[63]

Their luck was not good when the *Flyer* was finally ready for ground testing on November 5. The engine ran so rough that the vibrations damaged the propeller shafts. They would have to be sent back to Dayton to be repaired by Charley Taylor, a process guaranteed to take several weeks.

The setback could not have come at a worse time. Four days earlier Wilbur and Orville had learned that Langley was readying another attempt to fly his *Aerodrome.* They had no way of knowing if his machine was capable of flight, but it seemed likely he would get a second shot at history before they even got their first.

The situation caused Wilbur to make an uncharacteristically risky decision. He

STAY OR GO?

At this point, it would have been easy to give up. The weather was cold and miserable and now they faced another long delay. And for all they knew, Langley had already flown. But even after two months of frustration, there was little thought of quitting. While Wilbur waited at Kitty Hawk, Orville returned to Dayton to make new shafts of spring steel. When he returned on December 11 he had good news for Wilbur. Langley's second attempt had failed badly on December 8. If anyone was going to fly in 1903, it would be the Wright brothers.

The next day, they had the *Flyer* fully assembled, but the wind was too light to attempt a flight. Sunday, December 13, was out of the question since they had promised their father they would never work on a Sunday. Finally, on Monday afternoon the brothers ran a flag up on top of their work shed. It was a signal for the Kill Devil Hills Lifesaving Station. Any time they were about to make a flight they put out the flag so that any lifesavers not on duty could give them help.

Besides wanting as many witnesses as possible, the Wrights needed assistance in moving the heavy machine into position. Five men soon showed up to haul the *Flyer* a quarter mile to the slope of a sand dune. "We took to the hill," wrote Wilbur in a letter home that evening, "and after tossing for first whack [try], which I won, got ready for the start."[64]

Since the *Flyer* had no wheels and was too heavy for men to pick up and run with, the brothers had come up with a new way of launching it. The skids of the plane rested on a dolly whose wheels ran along the top of a primitive monorail made out of two-by-fours. Wilbur nicknamed it the "Junction Railroad."

By the time the *Flyer* reached the end of the track it was already six feet in the air. Then Wilbur made a mistake with the elevator. He turned the nose up too sharply causing the machine to lose its airspeed and lift. After only three-and-a-half seconds and 105 feet, the *Flyer* crashed. The left wing hit the ground first, swinging the plane around and breaking off one of the skids.

Wilbur was unhurt but no doubt a bit frustrated with himself. He had made only a "hop," not a real first flight. Still, he felt certain now that their machine would work as planned. Next morning he sent

Members of the Kill Devil Hills Lifesaving Station position the Flyer *for launch on December 14, 1903.*

Wilbur in the damaged Flyer *after an unsuccessful trial flight.*

a telegram to his father describing the flight. The last four words were: "SUCCESS ASSURED KEEP QUIET."[65]

SOARING INTO HISTORY

After repairing the plane, the brothers could hardly wait to get back in the air. But once again the weather refused to cooperate. Winds were too light until Thursday, December 17. Then, perversely, they were almost too strong. That morning was bitterly cold with a north wind blowing at nearly thirty miles per hour. Wilbur and Orville must have had an agonizing debate on whether to fly or not. It would likely be very dangerous.

But they were two months behind schedule and this wind might easily be-

come a storm lasting for weeks. If that happened, they would not get another chance until spring. They decided to go for it.

After summoning three lifesavers (two other observers also showed up), the launching track was laid down on the sand. Since the wind was so strong, there would be no need to launch from a slope. John Daniels was one of the lifesavers that day. He and the other men had doubts as to whether flying in such a strong wind was wise.

"We were a serious lot," he recalled twenty-fours years later. "Nobody felt like talking." It was Orville's turn to attempt flight and Daniels remembered how the brothers, too, seemed deeply concerned about the danger:

> Wilbur and Orville walked off from us and stood close together on the

beach, talking low to each other for some time. After a while they shook hands, and we couldn't help but notice how they held on to each other's hand, sort o'like they hated to let go; like two folks parting who weren't sure they'd ever see each other again.

Wilbur came over to us and told us not to look sad, but to laugh and . . . clap our hands and try to cheer Orville up when he started. We tried

to shout . . . but it was mighty weak shouting with no heart in it.[66]

With the witnesses waving halfheartedly, Orville released a restraining wire and the *Flyer* began moving down the track, its noisy engine clattering and vibrating. Wilbur ran alongside steadying the right wing. After only forty feet the *Flyer* rose into the air, dipped slightly, then rose again before settling gently to the sand some 120 feet from its starting

---

FIRST FLIGHT

Orville kept a diary while at Kitty Hawk. In this entry, reprinted in Miracle at Kitty Hawk *by Fred C. Kelly, he put down his recollections of mankind's first heavier-than-air flight. His mention of "trucks" refers to the little wheeled devices on which the* Flyer's *"sledlike skids" rested.*

"When we got up, a wind of between 20 and 25 miles was blowing from the north. We got the machine out early and put out the signal for the men at the station. . . . After running the engine and propellers a few minutes to get them in working order, I got on the machine at 10:35 for the first trial. . . . On slipping the rope the machine started off increasing in speed to probably 7 or 8 miles. The machine lifted from the truck just as it was entering on the fourth rail. Mr. Daniels took a picture just as it left the trucks.

I found the control of the front rudder quite difficult on account of its being balanced too near the center and thus had a tendency to turn itself when started so that the rudder was turned too far on one side and then too far on the other. As a result the machine would rise suddenly to about 10 feet and then as suddenly, on turning the rudder, dart for the ground. A sudden dart when out about 100 feet from the end of the track ended the flight."

Anatomy of a Historic Photograph

The photograph of Orville leaving the ground on December 17, 1903, is one of the most famous pictures of the twentieth century. In The Papers of Wilbur and Orville Wright, *Marvin W. McFarland describes in detail what the camera captured that morning.*

"Orville Wright is at the controls of the machine, lying prone on the lower wing with hips in the cradle which operated the wing-warping mechanism. Wilbur Wright, running alongside to balance the machine, has just released his hold on the forward upright of the right wing.

The horizontal front rudder is tilted up to what is probably its extreme position. The slow speed of the propellers (approximately five revolutions per second) is evident from the relatively small triangular blur caused by the rotating blades. The remarkably short length of the take-off into a wind of 20 to 27 miles per hour is apparent from the footprints in the sand, left of center, which outline the position of the right wing at the start of the flight.

The starting rail . . . was constructed of four 15-foot two-by-fours, topped with a thin metal strip. The truck which supported the skids of the plane during take-off is visible in the sand at the end of the starting rail. The truck consisted of two parts: the yoke, and an undercarriage which moved along the track on two rollers made from modified bicycle hubs.

point. After twelve seconds, the first airplane flight in history was over.

They Knew What They Had Done

Despite the flight's shortness, Wilbur and Orville had no doubt as to its importance. As Orville would write, "it was, nevertheless, the first in the history of the world in which a machine carrying a man had raised itself by its own power into the air in full flight, had sailed forward without reduction of speed, and had finally landed at a point as high as that from which it started."[67]

To document that historic moment, Orville had set up a camera on a tripod and asked John Daniels to snap the shutter when he became airborne. Daniel's picture showing Wilbur looking on just as the *Flyer* leaves the rail would become

The benchlike object in the foreground is the wing-rest to which the right wing was clamped to keep the machine from tipping when at rest. . . . The coil box that provided the initial spark in starting the motor is in front of the shovel. The connecting cables trail in the sand. Beyond the shovel is a can with nails, tacks, and a hammer in it, for emergency repairs.

Before the flight, Orville Wright set up his camera on a tripod between the camp buildings and the flying machine, adjusting the lens so that a point a few feet short of the end of the starting rail would fall on the center of the 5-by-7-inch glass plate. John T. Daniels of the Kill Devil Life Saving Station operated the shutter as the plane passed this point."

Wilbur looks on as Orville pilots the Flyer *during its first flight.*

one of the most famous photographs of the century.

Meanwhile, to prove the first flight was not a fluke, Wilbur and Orville flew three more times that day. On the last flight, Wilbur stayed in the air fifty-nine seconds while covering some 852 feet. Unfortunately, right afterwards a huge gust of wind caught the *Flyer*, tumbling it end over end. The machine was so badly damaged that it never flew again.

But the wreck could not dampen the brothers' spirits. As they packed up to head home for Christmas, it was clear they had built the world's first true flying machine. And they had no doubt they could do it again. That evening they sent a telegram home to Dayton. Although the telegraph operator misspelled Orville's name and the duration of the longest flight was given as 57 seconds instead of 59 seconds, the basic message was clear—they had flown at last!

6 Pioneers in the Pasture

Now that they had shown that a true flying machine could be built, the Wright brothers needed a place closer to home to practice flying it. They found that place just outside Dayton in 1904. For the next two years they refined their flying skills there. Meanwhile, patent considerations, their own stubbornness, and old-fashioned thinking by others prevented them from getting the recognition they deserved.

Although the Wrights were not publicity seekers, they never intended to keep their machine a secret. After all, the telegram they sent home on the evening of December 17 asked the family to inform the press. That job fell to their older brother Lorin and proved more difficult than they imagined. Seventy years later Lorin's daughter, Ivonette, could still remember the distressed look on her father's face when he returned from visiting the local office of the Associated Press. The editor there was annoyed at being bothered with such nonsense, "Fifty-seven seconds, hey? If it had been fifty-seven minutes then it might have been a news item."[68]

Eventually, some newspapers—even those in Dayton—reported reasonably accurate accounts of events at Kitty Hawk. But no one seemed to realize their impor-

tance. Few people then understood the difference between balloon flight and powered flight. At the time, news of spectacular balloon flights in Europe was still fresh in people's minds. And those flights were measured in hours—not seconds.

Another problem was that Samuel Langley's disastrous fifty-thousand dol-

Although receiving little recognition for their Flyer, *Orville (right) and Wilbur pressed on to develop a more practical flying machine.*

lar flop a month earlier seemed convincing proof of what so many experts had contended—a true heavier-than-air flying machine was simply an impossibility. It did not seem likely that two bicycle mechanics who had not finished high school and had no financial backing could succeed where one of the nation's most respected scientists had miserably failed.

While the patent situation remained unsettled, Wilbur and Orville were not greatly upset by the lack of publicity because it was less likely someone would hear about and steal their discoveries before they could be compensated. And, it gave them the freedom to perfect those discoveries in relative privacy.

The question of patents had become crucial because of a decision they made early in 1904. In a letter to an acquaintance Wilbur described their options.

> On the one hand we could continue playing with the problem of flying so long as youth and leisure would permit but carefully avoiding those features which would require continuous effort and the expenditure of considerable sums of money. On the other hand, we believed that if we would take the risk of devoting our entire time and financial resources we could conquer the difficulties in the path to success before increasing years impaired our physical ability.[69]

The brothers decided to commit all their time to the problem of flight. But since their financial future was at stake, they would regard their aviation work as a business proposition until they made

their money back. Both of them realized that flights of only fifty-nine seconds would not impress the world. If they were to make any money from their venture, they would have to build a practical aircraft. By January they were at work on a larger, more powerful machine.

PILOTS IN THE PASTURE

As mechanic Charley Taylor put it, "They wanted a new one built right away. They were always thinking of the next thing to do; they didn't waste much time thinking about the past."[70] Looking ahead to warm weather, they began searching for a place closer to home to practice their flying. They found it eight miles outside of town on a one hundred-acre farm pasture owned by Terrence Huffman. A local bank president, Huffman was not a believer in flight—he once told a nearby farmer that Wilbur and Orville were fools. Still, he offered them use of the land for free if they promised to shoo the cows and horses away first.

The spot, known as the Huffman Prairie, was far from perfect. It was about a quarter of a mile wide and a half a mile long and there were a few trees to avoid. With some exaggeration, Wilbur described it as an old swamp "filled with grassy hummocks some six inches high, so that it resembles a prairie dog town."[71]

But the Huffman Prairie site did have two major advantages. It was relatively isolated from prying eyes and it was on a trolley line only a short ride from West Dayton. In April the brothers began

Among Horses and Hummocks

The practice field at the Huffman Prairie was far from ideal. Wilbur listed its shortcomings in a letter he wrote to Octave Chanute on June 21, 1904. It was reprinted in Fred C. Kelly's Miracle at Kitty Hawk.

"You are quite right in thinking our Kitty Hawk grounds possess advantages not found at our present location, but we must learn to accommodate ourselves to circumstances. At Kitty Hawk we had unlimited space and wind enough to make starting easy with a short track. If the wind was very light we could utilize the hills if necessary in getting the initial velocity. Here we must depend on a long track, and light winds or even dead calms. We are in a large meadow . . . skirted on the west and north by trees. This not only shuts off the wind somewhat but also probably gives a slight down trend. . . . The greater troubles are . . . that in addition to cattle there have been a dozen or more horses in the pasture and as it is surrounded by barb wire fencing we have been at much trouble to get them safely away before making trials. Also the ground is an old swamp and is filled with grassy hummocks some six inches high so that it resembles a prairie dog town. This makes the track laying slow work. While we are getting ready the favorable opportunities slip away, and we are usually up against a rain storm, a dead calm, or a wind blowing at right angles to the track."

constructing a shed for their latest flying machine on a corner of the pasture. By late May the *Wright Flyer II* was completely assembled.

Realizing that any flights were bound to attract attention, Wilbur and Orville tried a different approach to head off the kinds of wild rumors that had sprung up after their Kitty Hawk flights. Some newspapers reported a three-mile flight and other false details like a six-bladed "underwheel" that pushed the machine up into the air. Other reporters had even signed Wilbur's name to interviews that had never occurred. The brothers were horrified by such dishonesty. That was why they invited reporters from newspapers in Dayton and Cincinnati to the

The Wright brothers with their second powered flying machine.

Huffman Prairie to witness them fly there on May 23. They did ask, however, that no photographs be taken and that the reports be factual.

On the appointed day a dozen reporters plus friends and family of the Wrights arrived to see the brothers in action. But it rained all morning, and then the wind died down. With only about a hundred feet of track it was nearly impossible to get the new *Flyer* airborne. Still, with so many people watching, the Wrights felt pressured to do something. They attempted a short hop, but the engine misfired and the *Flyer* slid off the end of the track without ever leaving the ground.

On the next day the reporters were invited back, but the weather would not cooperate. By Thursday only a few reporters were still interested enough to witness a hop of somewhere between twenty-five and sixty feet. It ended when the *Flyer* dropped suddenly to the ground, breaking several spars.

Although it could hardly be called a "flight," the Wrights were relieved that the reporters had written mostly favorable stories. "The fact that we are experimenting at Dayton is now public, but so far we have not been disturbed by visitors," Wilbur wrote to Chanute. "The newspapers are friendly and not disposed to arouse prying curiosity in the community."[72]

Wilbur was right about that—it would be sixteen months before another reporter visited the Huffman Prairie. The attitude of Luther Beard, who worked at the *Dayton Journal*, was typical. Beard sometimes rode the trolley with the Wrights and had even chatted with them. "I sort of felt sorry for them," he said. "They seemed like well-meaning decent young men. Yet there they were, neglecting their business to waste their time day after day on that ridiculous flying machine. I had an idea they must worry their father."[73]

NO MORE SOFT LANDINGS

In truth, their father did have plenty to worry about. The flights that summer were the most dangerous the brothers had ever attempted. No longer did they have the luxury of crashing into soft sand. And, although they did not know it at the time, the air in Dayton did not have the same lifting capacity as the denser air at sea level. The slightest drop in wind speed caused the underpowered *Flyer* to drop like a stone.

Again and again the brothers hit the ground hard. Nearly every crash added to the brother's collection of bumps and bruises, but they risked much worse. Takeoffs were especially dangerous. Charley Taylor said that every time he watched one of the brothers head down the rail, he wondered whether he might be seeing him alive for the last time. After Orville miraculously survived a particularly bad crash on August 24, the Wrights realized something had to be done.

Once again their mechanical abilities helped them devise an ingenious solution. They built a twenty-foot tower and hauled a sixteen hundred-pound weight to the top with pulleys. Other pulleys and ropes attached to the front of the plane. When the pilot was ready for takeoff he released a clip and the weight dropped, pulling the plane down the launching rail.

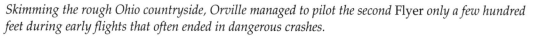

Skimming the rough Ohio countryside, Orville managed to pilot the second Flyer *only a few hundred feet during early flights that often ended in dangerous crashes.*

Workers tow the Flyer *to its launch tower. The catapult made for smoother takeoffs and longer, higher flights. It was a huge improvement.*

The new catapult launching system worked beautifully. Before September 7 they had made about forty flights, most of them two hundred feet or less. After the catapult was installed, they could fly the length of the field without difficulty. A week later they were making their first full turns in the air. And then, on September 20, a man named Amos Root witnessed history being made.

Root was publisher and editor of a beekeeping magazine. Fascinated by flight, he had driven 175 miles to check out the rumors of two young men flying in a cow pasture near Dayton. On the morning of September 20 he showed up and introduced himself to the brothers. His timing could not have been better.

That afternoon the *Flyer* made the first complete circle in aviation history.

Root was astonished. He called that four-thousand-foot flight "one of the grandest sights, if not the grandest sight, of my life." In an article later published in his magazine, he tried to describe what he had seen in a way his readers might understand:

> Imagine a locomotive that has left its track, and is climbing up in the air right toward you—a locomotive made of aluminum. Well now, imagine that locomotive with wings that spread 20 feet each way, coming right toward you with the tremendous flap of its propellers, and you have something like what I saw.[74]

Many more circles were flown after the one Root witnessed. Although Wilbur and Orville found the mechanics of turning difficult to master, they were learning more with every flight. By the time they stopped flying that December, flights were lasting up to five minutes.

By then Wilbur and Orville felt they had demonstrated that their invention was practical. It was time now to see whether they could sell it. As patriotic Americans, they wanted to offer the *Flyer* to their own government first.

Wilbur wrote a letter to the War Department telling how he and Orville had

---

It "Lands Without Being Wrecked"

Early in January 1905 Wilbur and Orville decided to offer their invention to the U.S. government. On January 18 they wrote this letter to their congressman. It was reprinted in Fred Kelly's Miracle at Kitty Hawk.

"The series of aeronautical experiments upon which we have been engaged for the past five years has ended in the production of a flying-machine of a type fitted for practical use. It not only flies through the air at high speed, but it also lands without being wrecked. During the year 1904 one hundred and five flights were made at our experimenting station on the Huffman prairie, east of the city; and though our experience in handling the machine has been too short to give any high degree of skill, we nevertheless succeeded, toward the end of the season, in making two flights of five minutes each, in which we sailed round and round the field until a distance of about three miles had been covered, at a speed of thirty-five miles an hour. The first of these record flights was made on November 9th . . . and the second, on December 1st, in honor of the one hundredth flight of the season.

The numerous flights in straight lines, in circles, and over "S"-shaped courses, in calms and in winds, have made it quite certain that flying has been brought to a point where it can be made of great practical use in various ways, one of which is that of scouting and carrying messages in time of war. . . .

If you can find it convenient to ascertain whether this is a subject of interest to our own government, it would oblige us greatly."

built a flying machine that had made two flights of five minutes each at thirty-five miles an hour. They offered to supply similar machines to the government as well as share the priceless aerodynamic knowledge they had acquired.

The War Department responded with a form letter saying that the government would not be interested until the machine had been "brought to the stage of practical operation."[75] Either no one had actually read the letter or whoever had read it did not believe Wilbur's account.

Disappointed, the Wrights then placed their hopes on negotiations with European governments. But negotiations with the British, and then the French, also eventually broke down. Wilbur and Orville still had not made a dime from all their work.

THE FIRST TRUE AIRPLANE

Despite the turndowns, the brothers were back flying at the Huffman Prairie in June of 1905. But on July 14 Orville had his worst crash ever, slamming into the ground at thirty miles per hour. The design changes made after that crash—the elevator was enlarged and moved farther forward—made the *Flyer* much safer. Most aviation experts regard the 1905 *Flyer* as the world's first practical aircraft.

Following the elevator improvements, the brothers flew greater and greater distances. But there was still one major control problem. During tight turns, the wing-warping controls sometimes failed to respond properly. A flight by Orville on September 28 provided a vital clue. While making a turn about fifty feet above the ground Orville realized he was headed for a honey locust tree.

He applied wing warping to veer away, but nothing happened. Figuring his only chance was to land immediately, he turned the nose of the *Flyer* sharply down. As he did so, the wing warping suddenly worked again and the aircraft turned away from the tree.

After Orville landed, he and Wilbur talked over what had happened. They soon realized that, during tight turns, centrifugal force was slowing down the inside wing to the point where it no longer had enough lift. "When we had discovered the real nature of the problem," wrote Wilbur, "and knew that it could always be remedied by tilting the machine forward a little, so that its flying

Orville pilots the 1905 Flyer, *considered the world's first practical aircraft by many aviation experts.*

speed would be restored, we felt that we were ready to place flying machines on the market."[76]

With this newfound knowledge, flight time increased greatly. On October 3 the *Flyer* made a twenty-six-minute flight. Two days later Wilbur stayed aloft for thirty-nine minutes, circling the field thirty times and covering about twenty-four miles. Amos Stauffer, a farmer working in a nearby field was amazed: "I just kept on shocking [stacking] corn until I got down to the fence. And the durned thing was still going round. I thought it would never stop."[77]

Lying in the prone position for that long was very uncomfortable. Years later Orville told biographer Fred C. Kelly how he used to think the back of his neck would break if he endured one more turn around the field.

By this time their flights were creating such a sensation that newspapers could no longer ignore them. When stories began appearing again, the brothers abruptly stopped flying. They felt they

FACT OR FABLE?

Even in 1906, more than two years after the Wright brothers' first flight, hardly anyone believed their claims. Fred C. Kelly, in Miracle at Kitty Hawk, *points out that even supposedly scientific observers dismissed factual reports without even bothering to check them out.*

"The *Scientific American* of January 13, 1906, in an article headed 'The Wright Aeroplane and Its Fabled Performances,' commented skeptically on a letter written by the Wright brothers which had been published in a Paris automobile journal. In that letter the Wrights had given details of the long flights of late September and early October, 1905. In expressing its disbelief in the 'alleged' flights described in the Wright letter, the *Scientific American* said: 'If such sensational and tremendously important experiments are being conducted in a not very remote part of the country, on a subject in which almost everybody feels the most profound interest, is it possible to believe that the enterprising American reporter, who, it is well known, comes down the chimney when the door is locked in his face—even if he has to scale a fifteen-story skyscraper to do so—would not have ascertained all about them and published them . . . long ago?'"

Alberto Santo-Dumont at the controls of his "heavier-than-air machine."

had little left to prove. They could take off and land safely, stay aloft for hours and control their craft in flight. Yet, without a patent, release of detailed information about their invention could only hurt them financially.

They would retire from flying until a buyer came forward. Their wait would last close to two-and-a-half years. During that time their claims were greeted with great skepticism, especially in France, then considered the center of aeronautical knowledge.

FLYERS OR LIARS?

In Europe, balloons and flying machines were only built by the wealthy. Since the Wright brothers were not rich, people wondered who had financed their experiments. It just did not seem possible they could have done so themselves.

People also wondered why, if they had really flown, there was so little about it in the U.S. newspapers. Surely, reporters would have been rushing to Dayton to cover such a huge story. The consensus in France was that the Wright's claims were exaggerations.

The brothers' secretiveness also hurt them in their business dealings. Unwilling to trust others, they refused to share details about their machine until a contract was signed. As honest men, they did not see that as a problem—after all, if they did not fulfill the terms of the contract they would not get their money. But they failed to realize that government bureaucrats risked great ridicule if they were thought to be wasting time on something most people regarded as foolish.

In retrospect, the brothers could have saved themselves years of frustration if they had made a public flight demonstration. At that point, governments probably would have lined up to buy their invention. But Wilbur and Orville thought they had an unbeatable lead in building functional aircraft. "We do not believe there is one chance in a hundred that any one will have a machine of the least practical significance within five years,"[78] wrote Wilbur on October 10, 1906.

They were wrong. Thirteen days later, Alberto Santo-Dumont, a Brazilian living in Paris, created a stir by flying nearly two hundred feet in a heavier-than-air machine. A few weeks later, he flew 726 feet. His machine was primitive com-

Frenchman Henri Farman completed a successful trial of his own flying machine in November 1906.

pared to the Wrights, but its flights caused great excitement in France.

A year later Leon Delagrange flew sixteen thousand feet and on November 18 Henri Farman flew an almost complete circle while covering nearly a mile outside Paris. Orville, in France trying to sign a contract with the government, was a witness that day. He could see that he and Wilbur were still far ahead of everyone else, but he had no way then of proving it. It must have been even more frustrating when he learned how French flyers compared their accomplishments with the Wrights'. Most believed the brothers were fakes.

The frustration finally ended a month later. By then even the U.S. government realized that a new era of flight was dawning. Just before Christmas they put out a public bid for a heavier-than-air flying machine. The bidding was mostly a formality since the army officers who had investigated knew that only Wilbur and Orville could fulfill the terms.

More good news came in March when the Wrights signed a deal with a group of French businessmen to provide them with planes. Demonstrations were scheduled that summer in both the United States and in France. If the Wright planes could meet the performance standards set in the contracts, the brothers would be in business.

At last they were going to be able to show the world what they had accomplished. But after a two-and-a-half-year layoff, they needed to brush up on their flying skills.

Chapter

7 The Bird Men of 1908

1908 was a breakthrough year for the Wrights. With a series of spectacular flights on either side of the Atlantic, Wilbur and Orville proved their mastery of the air. In the process, they stunned their critics into silence, astonished the world and became the century's first international celebrities.

All of that was ahead of them in April when they returned once again to the Outer Banks. Following their self-imposed vacation from flying, they desperately needed practice time in the air. Their new machine featured a more powerful engine and upright seating, but it would undoubtedly take some time to learn how the new control levers handled.

By early May the brothers had their old camp at Kill Devil Hills rebuilt and were ready to test their new machine. On May 6 Wilbur rolled down the takeoff rail and flew one thousand feet—his first time in the air since 1905. Two days later the brothers made several long flights after lunch.

Bruce Salley, a reporter for the *Norfolk Landmark*, was hiding in the dunes nearby. He had assumed the brothers would not fly if they knew reporters were watching. Actually, the brothers knew they were being watched and were somewhat amused by all the sneaking around.

Astounded by the first flight he saw, Salley forgot all about hiding and ran over to the Wright's camp to ask for more information. His reports led the the *New York Herald* to send one of its best reporters, Byron Newton, to North Carolina to investigate.

Newton was not pleased with the assignment. He doubted the Wrights had ever really flown and the backwardness of the local residents did not impress him either. They were, he said, "well nigh as ignorant of the modern world as if they lived in the depths of Africa."[79]

On the morning of May 11 Newton and several other reporters crept into hiding places near the Wrights' camp. They could see the doors of the shed open and outside it, the flying machine balanced on its launching rail. Three men—Wilbur, Orville, and Charlie Furnas, a mechanic friend from Dayton—could be seen working on the machine.

Then one of them climbed into the pilot seat while the others kept fiddling with the engine. What Newton saw next changed his attitude forever.

For some minutes the propeller blades continued to flash in the sun, and then the machine rose obliquely

The Guns Were Imaginary

The newspaper reporters sneaking around outside the Wright brothers' camp at Kitty Hawk in 1908 might have learned a lot more if they had just walked into camp. However, among the wild rumors that had circulated about the secretive Wrights was one that claimed they guarded their discoveries with firearms. In this excerpt from Miracle at Kitty Hawk, *Fred C. Kelly reveals what Wilbur and Orville really thought of the spies they knew were prowling about.*

"'What would you have done,' Orville Wright was asked afterward, 'if all those correspondents had come right to your camp each day and sat there to watch you?'

'We'd have had to go ahead just as if they weren't there,' he replied. 'We couldn't have delayed our work. There was too much to do and our time was short.'

That the Wrights would have treated the correspondents politely enough was indicated in a letter from Orville Wright to Byron Newton, dated June 7, 1908. Immediately after his return to New York, Newton had written graciously to the Wrights, enclosing clippings of his dispatches to the *Herald* and expressing his admiration for them and their achievements.

'We were aware of the presence of newspapermen in the woods,' Orville wrote, 'at least we had often been told that they were there. Their presence, however, did not bother us in the least, and I am only sorry that you did not come over to see us at our camp. The display of a white flag would have disposed of the rifles and shotguns with which the machine is reported to have been guarded.'"

into the air. At first it came directly toward us, so that we could not tell how fast it was going except that it appeared to increase rapidly in size as it approached. In the excitement of this first flight, men trained to observe details under all sorts of distractions, forgot their cameras, forgot their watches, forgot everything but this aerial monster chattering over our heads. As it neared us we could plainly see the operator in his seat working at the upright levers close by his side. When it was almost squarely over us there was a movement of the forward and rear guiding planes . . . and the

The 1905 Wright Flyer *on the launching track at Kill Devil Hills in 1908.*

machine wheeled about at an angle every bit as gracefully as an eagle flying close to the ground.[80]

Newton witnessed Orville making a flight of about a half mile. Afterwards he described the experience as "different from the contemplation of any other marvel human eyes may behold in a life time."[81]

May 14 proved to be the Wright brothers best—and last—day of flying on the Outer Banks in 1908. In the morning Charlie Furnas rode along as a passenger on the first two-man flights in history. After dinner Wilbur made the longest flight ever in North Carolina, covering five miles.

FAREWELL TO KITTY HAWK

But the flight ended abruptly when Wilbur accidentally turned the elevator handle the wrong way and plowed into the sand at fifty miles an hour. Dazed and bruised, he somehow escaped serious injury. However, the plane's upper wing was ruined.

Meanwhile, a telegram from France made it clear that a demonstration there

Big Brother Was Not Happy!

In June 1908 the crate with the Flyer *arrived in Europe from America. As Marvin W. McFarland notes in this excerpt from* The Papers of Wilbur and Orville Wright, *Wilbur could barely control his anger. He thought Orville had packed the crate haphazardly, but what really had happened was that French customs officials had torn everything apart. Wilbur's response amused Orville and for years he kept a copy of it to show friends an example of how a "kid brother" sometimes gets treated.*

"I opened the boxes yesterday and have been puzzled ever since to know how you could have wasted two whole days packing them. I am sure that with a scoop shovel I could have put things in within two or three minutes and made fully as good a job of it. . . . Did you tell Charley not to separate anything lest it should get lonesome? Ten or a dozen ribs were broken and as they are scattered here and there through the surfaces, it takes almost as much time to tear down and rebuild as if we could have begun at the beginning. One surface was so bad that I took it completely down. Never again pack anything else in the surface box. The cloth is torn in almost numberless places and the aluminum has rubbed off the skid sticks and dirtied the cloth very badly. The radiators are badly mashed; the seat is broken; the magneto has the oil cap broken off, the coils badly torn up, and I suspect the axle is bent a little, the tubes of the screw supports are mashed and bent. . . .

To be brief, things must be packed at least ten times as well as they were last time. And everything must be listed and the net weights taken off the stuff in each box.

In looking over the materials I notice that the rear wire is sometimes not inside both cloths; there are no blocks to keep the end ribs on each section from slipping inward when the surfaces are taken apart; the little washer on the rear wire is on the wrong side of the rib and therefore useless; the rear spar is not wrapped with glued cloth where the screw frames fasten on, and the screws are only 1 inch instead of 1-1/4 inch as heretofore. . . . We have been delayed because we have been unable as yet to get anything to replace them. It is going to take much longer for me to get ready than it should have done if things had been in better shape."

would have to be arranged immediately. If not, the deal might fall through. With two contracts to worry about at the same time, the brothers had no choice but to split up. Wilbur headed for New York directly from Kitty Hawk, while Orville hurried back to Dayton to prepare a machine for the army tests.

From New York Wilbur took a steamer to Europe, arriving in Paris on May 29. He was unhappy with what he found there. The French company they had hired to assemble engines for them was totally incompetent. The engines they had built were mechanical horrors and they had even severely damaged an original motor sent over to use as a model.

Wilbur had an even more unpleasant surprise when he opened the packing crate containing the *Flyer's* airframe. Orville had

sent it over from Dayton, but French customs officials had so carelessly repacked it after inspection that nearly every part of the plane had been damaged.

Unable to communicate with the French mechanics assisting him, Wilbur had no choice but to rebuild the engine and the *Flyer* all by himself. That became even more difficult after July 4 when a radiator hose split during an engine test, spraying his chest and left arm with scalding water. Although severely burned, Wilbur continued with his work.

The Pressure Mounts

Meanwhile, the pressure to hurry was increasing. French newspapers almost daily carried news of French aviators like

Wilbur Wright's 1907 model A biplane draws a curious crowd in Le Mans, France.

Wilbur Wright prepares the Flyer *for its first flight demonstration in Le Mans.*

Voisin and Farman. That summer Leon Delagrange flew nine miles in eighteen-and-a-half minutes. Wilbur and Orville knew that the French were years behind them in flight control. Only one of them had even flown in a crude circle.

But the rest of the world did not know that. There was pride in French accomplishments and much skepticism about the Wrights. Magazines called them "bluffers" and "bicycle peddlers." Finally on Saturday, August 8, Wilbur was ready to make his first public flight at Les Hunaudieres, an automobile racetrack near Le Mans. There would be only twenty-six spectators—but they were an influential group of French aviators, aviation buffs, and reporters.

It is hard to imagine now the kind of pressure Wilbur Wright was under that day. This particular machine had never flown and the controls had never been tested in flight. Yet any kind of simple mistake—like moving a lever in the wrong direction—could easily lead to a crash. Wilbur was not only risking his life, but the Wright brothers' reputation. An unsuccessful flight would only confirm the widespread belief that the Wrights were imposters.

Around half past six in the evening Wilbur took his seat on the lower wing and the engine was started. Then, with the propellers turning and the engine clattering, the weights beneath the tower were released and the *Flyer* began moving down the track. Used to long, lumbering takeoffs, the spectators were astonished at how quickly the machine sprang into the air.

But their cheers quickly turned into cries of alarm as the *Flyer* headed straight for a stand of trees at the end of the track. French planes needed lots of room to attempt a turn. Most observers were convinced they were about to see a crash. But Wilbur banked the plane sharply and continued down the other side of the

The Wright Flyer *soars into the air over the racetrack at Le Mans.*

racetrack. He was showing a kind of control that no one watching had dreamed possible.

"WE ARE AS CHILDREN"

After two complete circuits of the field Wilbur gently brought the *Flyer* down only fifty feet from where he had started. The stunned and amazed spectators surged out of the grandstand shouting and laughing with amazement. Many tried to hug and kiss Wilbur who, although he did not show it, was extremely relieved. Later he admitted he had made at least ten mistakes but had corrected them so quickly no one noticed.

The French airmen had little doubt of the importance of what they had seen. "I consider that for us in France, and everywhere, a new era in mechanical flight has commenced. I am not sufficiently calm after the event to thoroughly express my opinion," said a stunned Louis Blériot. "The whole conception of the machine—its execution and its practical worth—is wonderful," enthused René Gasnier. "We are as children compared to the Wrights."[82]

After Wilbur landed safely, Henri Delgove, a thirteen-year-old who had been watching with his friend, could contain his excitement no longer. Hopping on their bicycles, the two boys pedaled into Le Mans shouting, "He flies—he flies—he's no liar, he's a flier!"[83]

Almost overnight, the expression "birdmen" become a way to describe the Wright brothers' seemingly miraculous abilities. Word of the events at Les Hunaudieres spread quickly. When Wilbur flew again on Monday, a crowd of over two thousand was on hand. He made two flights that day, the second one featuring a figure eight—a maneuver no one else had ever attempted before.

"COURTESY HAS LIMITS"

By the end of August 1908 Wilbur's flights in France were attracting worldwide attention, reports Fred C. Kelly in Miracle at Kitty Hawk. *In this letter sent to Orville on August 25, Wilbur describes the scene at Le Mans and, like a true older brother, stresses his concern that Orville keep safety his foremost concern.*

A struggle between the curious public and the cautious Wright brothers sometimes kept their flying machines "grounded".

"The excitement aroused by the short flights I have made is almost beyond comprehension. The French have simply become wild. Instead of doubting that we could do anything they are ready to believe that we can do everything. So the present situation is almost as troublesome as the former one. People have flocked here from all over Europe, and as I wish to practice rather than give exhibitions it is a little embarrassing. But I tell them plainly that I intend for the present to experiment only under the most favorable conditions. If the wind is more than five miles an hour I stay in. In a calm you can detect a mismovement instantly, but in winds you do not know at first whether the trouble is due to mistakes or to wind gusts. I advise you most earnestly to stick to calms till after you are sure of yourself. Don't go out even for all the officers of the government unless you would go equally if they were absent. *Do not let yourself be forced into doing anything before you are ready.* Be very cautious and proceed slowly in attempting flights in the middle of the day when wind gusts are frequent. Let it be understood that you wish to practice rather than give demonstrations and that you intend to do it in your own way. Do not let people talk to you all day and all night. It will wear you out, before you are ready for real business. Courtesy has limits. If necessary appoint some hour in the day time and refuse absolutely to receive visitors even for a minute at other times. Do not receive *any one* after 8 o'clock at night . . . .

It is not probable that I will be able to go to Washington unless absolutely needed. I can only say be extraordinarily cautious. Choose your own times. Good luck."

It created a sensation. "It is marvelous, I assure you, marvelous," was the comment of aviator Leon Delagrange. Later, he admitted to a reporter, "We are beaten."[84]

WORD OF A "WONDERFUL FLYING-MACHINE"

The crowds grew bigger each day as Wilbur's feats captured the attention of the world. "THE MOST WONDERFUL FLYING-MACHINE THAT HAS EVER BEEN MADE" was the headline in the London *Daily Mirror*. A reporter for *Le Figaro*, a French newspaper, could barely control his enthusiasm. "I've seen him: I've seen them! Yes! I have today seen Wilbur Wright and his great white bird, the beautiful mechanical bird . . . there is no doubt! Wilbur and Orville Wright have well and truly flown."[85]

Wilbur flew eight more times between Monday and Thursday of that week. Each time the crowds grew larger and more excited. Because he was still trying to familiarize himself with the controls, he did not stay in the air long. He was afraid the constant cheering would cause him to lose his concentration and make a mistake.

The Wright military airplane being transported to Fort Myer, Virginia for Orville's demonstration flights.

No One to Depend On

Although proud of Orville's first flights at Fort Myer, the stress Wilbur was feeling —both for himself and for Orville's safety—was growing. In this letter, sent to his sister on September 10 and reprinted here from Fred C. Kelly's Miracle at Kitty Hawk, *he confesses to being nearly overwhelmed.*

"I received word last evening of Orville's flight of 57 minutes, and today learn of his having passed the hour in a second flight later in the day. It is a record for sure! I have not done much for several weeks, partly because of windy weather, partly because of accidents which have necessitated repairs, and partly because I have been so nervous and worried that I have not felt like doing much hustling. You can scarcely imagine what a strain it is on one to have no one you can depend on to understand what you say, and want done, and what is more, no one capable of doing the grade of work we have always insisted upon in our machines. It compels me to do almost everything myself and keeps me worried."

On Thursday he did make a mistake. Forced to land because he lost too much airspeed making a tight turn, he did not have room to level out. The *Flyer*'s left wing smashed into the ground. Wilbur was unhurt, but a few days were needed for repairs. The time off gave Wilbur a chance to write to Orville:

The newspapers and the French aviators nearly went wild with excitement. Bléirot & Delagrange were so excited they could scarcely speak, and Kapferer could only gasp and could not talk at all. You would have almost died of laughter if you could have seen them. The French newspapers . . . gave reports fully as favorable as the *Herald*. You never saw anything like the complete reversal of position that took place after two or three little flights of less than two minutes each.[86]

Orv's Amazing Show

Although heartened by Wilbur's success in Europe, Orville was too busy with his own challenges to dwell on it. He arrived at Fort Myer, Virginia, on August 20 to begin preparations for the tests with the army. The flights would be made on a parade ground just west of Arlington National Cemetery.

Late in the afternoon of September 3 the *Flyer* was placed on the launching rails. Before a sizable crowd, including President Theodore Roosevelt's twenty-year-old son, Orville took to the air. He reached a height of thirty-five feet and was making his second circuit of the field when he made a mistake and had to bring the plane down hard to prevent a crash. The flight lasted only seventy-one seconds and did not even rate front-page coverage in the Washington newspapers.

Unlike the French observers, most American reporters had never seen a plane in flight. They did not realize how much mastery it took to make the tight turns that Orville demonstrated in his short flight. The crowds were gone when Orville flew again, early in the morning of September 9. They missed a world record, as he stayed aloft for fifty-seven and one-half minutes.

Next day the crowds were back to see him break the record again with a flight of sixty-two and one-half minutes. He also flew for six minutes with a passenger, setting another record in that category also. Over a period of four days Orville would set nine world records, including one for an altitude of 310 feet.

By this time newspapers were beginning to realize that aviation history was being made on both sides of the Atlantic. Stories began to appear suggesting that the brothers were competing with each other to set records. Wilbur good-naturedly remarked on it in a letter to Orville:

The newspapers for several days have been full of the stories of your dandy

Lieutenant Thomas Selfridge (seated) and Orville Wright just before the fatal flight of September 17, 1908.

Orville was buried inside the wreckage of this Fort Myer crash. He survived, but his passenger did not.

flights, and whereas a week ago I was a marvel of skill now they do not hesitate to tell me that I am nothing but a "dud" and they say you are the only genuine skyscraper. Such is fame! Your flights have naturally created an immense sensation in Europe and I suppose that America is nearly as wild.[87]

MANNED FLIGHT'S FIRST FATALITY

Orville's flights came to an abrupt and disastrous end on the afternoon of September 17. Lieutenant Thomas Selfridge was along as a passenger and they had just made three circuits of the field when Orville heard a mysterious tapping sound. A few seconds later there were two loud thumps and the *Flyer* began shaking violently. On the ground, spectators saw something fly from the plane and fall to earth.

Orville shut off the engine and tried to land, but the plane snapped over into a vertical dive and hit the ground with a sickening thud. When the dust cleared both Orville and Selfridge lay buried in the wreckage. Unconscious and bleeding, Orville was removed first. Convinced that his boss was dead, Charley Taylor started to cry.

But Orville was still alive. Although he had a broken left thigh, broken ribs, scalp wounds, and an injured back, he would recover. Selfridge, however, never regained consciousness. He has the dubious honor of being the first person to ever die in an airplane accident.

"The Machine Would Not Respond"

Two weeks after he was released from the hospital Orville wrote Wilbur with his account of the accident that killed Lieutenant Selfridge. Fred C. Kelly includes the letter in Miracle at Kitty Hawk. *All had been going well when, suddenly, a slight tapping was heard from the rear of the machine. Two seconds later, it was followed by two loud thumps.*

"The machine suddenly turned to the right and I immediately shut off the power. I then discovered that the machine would not respond to the steering and lateral balancing levers, which produced a most peculiar feeling of helplessness. Yet I continued to push the levers, when [with] the machine's sudden turn to the left, (the right wing rising high in the air) . . . it faced directly up the field. I reversed the levers to stop the turning and to bring the wings on a level. Quick as a flash, the machine turned down in front and started straight for the ground . . . .

Lieutenant Selfridge up to this time had not uttered a word, though he took a hasty glance behind when the propeller broke, and turned once or twice to look into my face, evidently to see what I thought of the situation. But when the machine turned head first for the ground, he exclaimed 'Oh! Oh!' in an almost inaudible voice.

I pulled the front rudder lever to its limit, but there was no response in the course of the machine. Thinking that, maybe, something was caught and that the rudder was not completely turned, I released the lever a little and gave another pull, but there was no change . . . . The first 50 ft. of that plunge seemed like a half minute, though I can hardly believe that it was over one second at most. The front rudder in that distance had not changed course more than five or ten degrees. Suddenly just before reaching the ground, probably 25 feet, something changed—the machine began to right itself rapidly. A few feet more, and we would have landed safely."

When news reached Wilbur he canceled all flying for a week and set off for Le Mans on his bicycle to await further news by telegram. He was convinced that the accident was his fault. As the responsible older brother, he was convinced that

Orville must have overlooked some detail that he would have caught.

"I cannot help thinking over and over again, 'If I had been there, it would not have happened,'" he wrote Katharine. "The worry over leaving Orville alone to undertake those trials was one of the chief things in almost breaking me down a few weeks ago and as soon as I heard reassuring news from America I was well again."[88]

As it turned out, the accident was not Orville's fault. A propeller blade had broken off and set up such a violent vibration that a wire connected to the rudder had come loose. Despite the crash, the army was impressed with what they had seen. "Of course we deplore the accident," said George Squier, "but no one who saw the flight of the last four days at Fort Myer could doubt for an instant that the problem of aerial navigation was solved."[89] The army gave the Wrights a nine-month extension to fulfill their contract.

Assured that Orville would recover, Wilbur began flying again. He had moved his base of operations to Camp d'Avours, about seven miles east of Le Mans. The French army artillery range there offered him greater room, but it meant greater crowds, too. On September 21, before a cheering crowd of ten thousand, he set a new endurance record with a flight of an hour and thirty-one minutes. "This will cheer Orville up a bit,"[90] he said as he stepped from his plane.

8 Fame and Misfortune

By the fall of 1908 the entire civilized world was captivated by the achievements of the Wright brothers. Curiosity about these two quiet men from Dayton was at a fever pitch. Then, a series of spectacular demonstrations in Europe in 1909 drew even more attention.

In America that summer, Orville fulfilled the conditions of the army contract, guaranteeing financial security for the brothers. A few months later, before millions of witnesses, Wilbur made two of the most dramatic and influential flights in history, demonstrating once and for all that heavier-than-air flight was practical.

Fame did not come easy to either brother, but Wilbur may have suffered most. In an era when only wealthy men had the time and money to devote to flying, he was a great puzzle to the French. He did not seem to care what other people thought of him. And, while the rich and famous were naturally eager to meet him, his humility endeared him to all.

While putting together the *Flyer* at Leon Bollee's automobile factory in Le Mans he worked in overalls. When the noon whistle blew he ate lunch along with the other workmen. Although they had trouble communicating with him, Bollee's workers developed great regard for Wilbur.

"Veelbur Reet" was how they pronounced his name. Coincidentally, the French words for "old oilcan" are *vielle burette*. That, plus Wilbur's unassuming ways, led to his affectionate nickname, "Old Oilcan."[91]

People could not understand why such a famous man would choose to sleep in an airplane hangar next to his plane, his only companion a stray dog he had named *Flyer.* Crowds followed him everywhere, hoping for a glimpse of the wizard who had unlocked the secrets of flight. One of the few places Wilbur could get any privacy was inside the hangar where his plane was kept. Even then, people drilled holes in the walls to get a peek at him.

Nowhere to Hide

In a letter to Octave Chanute, Wilbur complained, "For three months I have had scarcely a moment to myself except when I take my bicycle and ride off into the woods for a little rest. How I long for Kitty Hawk!"[92]

For such a private man, the constant attention was nearly intolerable. "I get so angry at the continual annoyance of hav-

"LIKE A BOAT RISING TO A BIG WAVE"

As president of the Aeronautical Society of Great Britain, Major Baden Fletcher Smyth Baden-Powell had an avid interest in aviation. While Wilbur was at Le Mans Baden-Powell asked to be given a ride in the Flyer. *His account of what it was like to fly with Wilbur Wright appeared in Tom Crouch's* The Bishop's Boys.

"Then the driver bends down and releases the catch which holds the anchoring wire. The machine is off! It bounds forward and travels rapidly along the rail. The foreplanes are meanwhile pressed down to prevent the machine lifting prematurely, but when about half the length of the rail has been traversed, the lever is pulled back, the planes come into operation, and the whole machine rises almost imperceptibly off the track. The ascent must be very gradual. When the machine leaves the track it glides so close to the ground that one often doubts if it is really started in the air, but then it gradually mounts. . . .

So steady and regular is the motion that it appears exactly as if it were progressing along an invisible elevated track. Only just now and again, as a swirl of wind catches it, does it make a slight undulation like a boat rising to a big wave. Mr. Wright, with both hands grasping the levers, watches every move, but his movements are so slight as to be almost imperceptible. Having soon reached the end of the ground, the machine is guided round in a semicircle, gracefully leaning over as it turns. . . .

All the time the engine is buzzing so loudly and the propellers humming so that after a trip one is almost deaf."

ing the crowd about that I feel like quitting the whole thing and going home," Wilbur wrote his father, "but when I think of the sacrifices some of them have made in the hope of seeing a flight I cannot help feeling sorry for them when I do not go out."[93]

Fortunately for the crowds, Wilbur flew often that fall. Besides setting numerous world records for time and altitude, he carried more than forty passengers during his stay at Le Mans. Among them was his agent's wife, Mrs. Hart Berg. The first woman to fly, she helped Wilbur start a fashion trend.

Before taking off she tied a cord around her skirt to keep it from blowing

Wilbur Wright took numerous passengers on flights, including Mrs. Hart Berg, the first woman to fly.

in the wind. After they landed, she hobbled away from the *Flyer* for a few steps before removing the cord. Because a dress designer happened to be a spectator that day, the fashion world was introduced to hobble skirts a few weeks later.

It was not the only fad Wilbur's popularity helped spark. While in Europe he always wore a distinctive green cloth cap. After his famous flights, thousands of such caps, called "Veelburs," were sold all over France.

At the very end of the year Wilbur notified the French that he would try for the Michelin prize awarded for the longest flight of 1908. He confidently waited until the final day of December so that no one would have any chance to beat him. With snow on the ground and the temperature below freezing, Wilbur took off from Camp d'Avours on the morning of December 31.

A broken fuel line ended that flight after forty-two minutes, but in the afternoon a bundled-up Wilbur flew around the frigid course for as long as he could stand it—two hours and eighteen minutes. Not only was the prize of twenty thousand francs his, but the French government announced that he and his brother would be presented with the Legion of Honor.

REUNIONS AND ROYALTY

Chances are that Wilbur was less excited about that award than he was about seeing familiar faces again. On January 12, after crossing the Atlantic by ship, Katharine and Orville joined Wilbur in Paris. Orville was now able to walk with the help of two canes. The family reunion, however, was a short one. On the next day Wilbur left for Pau in the south of France (Katharine and Orville rejoined him after a few days in Paris).

As part of his contract he had agreed to train three French pilots. The weather at Pau was much milder and the field was the best Wilbur had ever seen—plenty of room and almost no trees. During February and March Wilbur made some sixty flights, most of them with his student pilots. He, Orville, and Katharine were also visited by kings, prime ministers, dukes, duchesses, and generals. As Wilbur put it, "Princes and millionaires are as thick as fleas."[94] Even Katharine became a celebrity, but as always, Wilbur drew the most attention. There was something about his hawklike features and penetrating gaze that made a lasting impression.

After his last flight near Pau on March 20, Wilbur headed for Rome. For ten thousand dollars he had agreed to provide the aeronautical society there with a plane and teach an operator its use. The plane

Wilbur (left) and Orville Wright walking in Pau, France in the spring of 1908.

had been shipped to Rome earlier. Soon after his arrival, Wilbur was introduced to King Victor Emmanuel of Italy. Never overly impressed with royalty, Wilbur wrote in a letter to Orville the next day that when the king sat in a chair, his feet failed to reach the floor by about a foot.

During his four weeks in Rome Wilbur flew from a field named Centocelle. Away from Dayton for nearly a year, he was beginning to get homesick. At Centocelle he took his meals with some Italian officers stationed nearby and, by his reckoning, consumed "47 miles of macaroni."[95] After finishing their Italian obligations, the Wrights attended a farewell banquet at Le Mans and re-

ceived more awards in London before taking a ship to New York.

A Pair of Reluctant Heroes

They had hoped to come home to Dayton without a lot of fuss, but they were now internationally famous. Ten thousand people were waiting when their train pulled into the station. Factory whistles blew and cannons boomed as the Wrights were escorted from the depot in a carriage pulled by four white horses.

That was only the beginning. During a two-day celebration on June 17 and 18 General James Allen presented Wilbur

Wilbur prepares for a demonstration at Fort Myer in one of the brothers' military planes.

and Orville with Congressional Medals of Honor. The brothers hated such affairs, especially since it gave them even less time to get the army's *Flyer* ready for its trials later that month.

They worked on the plane during every spare moment, hanging canvas over the windows of their bicycle shop to block out the staring crowds. They managed to get it ready in time for launching at Fort Myer on June 28. It was arranged that Orville would do the flying while Wilbur made certain the machine was in good mechanical condition.

Unfortunately, the trials got off to a rocky start. The first flights lasted only seconds and some takeoffs did not get off the ground at all. There were problems with the engine and two minor crashes as Orville learned the controls. One flight of nine minutes was made, but on another flight Orville had to land when the motor died. When the right wing caught a small tree and both skids collapsed, he was badly shaken but not seriously hurt.

After the plane was repaired, bad weather and more mechanical problems kept any flying to a minimum. Finally on July 17 Orville circled the field for seventeen minutes. Three days later he broke the U.S. endurance record with a flight of one hour and twenty minutes. He also performed three figure eights and climbed to three hundred feet.

By this time all of Washington was aware of what was going on across the Potomac. Big crowds began showing up to watch Orville fly. On July 26, before President Taft and an audience of about ten thousand, Orville attempted to fulfill the part of the contract that called for him to fly for an hour with a passenger.

HONKING FOR ORVILLE

Lieutenant Frank Lahm climbed into the passenger seat at 6:35 that evening, well aware that the last man in his position had died in a horrible crash. But this time Orville stayed aloft for an hour and twelve minutes, breaking the world record held by Wilbur. As the last seconds ticked away, people cheered, car horns honked, and the usually calm Wilbur even did a little dance in the middle of the field.

The other part of the contract called for a two-man cross-country flight of ten miles; something no one had ever attempted. The Wrights decided to fly to Shuter's Hill in Alexandria, Virginia, and back. Because he only weighed 126 pounds, Lieutenant Benny Foulois was chosen as the passenger. After takeoff on July 30 Orville flew two circles of the parade ground to gain altitude, then headed over the treetops toward Alexandria. Foulois later recalled:

The air was bumpy, and I had the feeling that there were moments when Orville didn't have full control of the machine as we dipped groundward. It was as if someone on the ground had a string attached to us and would pull it occasionally as they would a kite. But each time Orville would raise the elevators slightly, and we would gain back the lost altitude.[96]

Orville Wright and Lieutenant Lahm making the world's record flight at Fort Myer on July 26, 1909.

Earlier, Orville had told him that if there was any trouble he would land in a field or "the thickest clump of trees I can find."[97] After rounding Shuter's Hill, Orville climbed to four hundred feet (a new altitude record) so that he could dive down and pick up speed as he raced toward the finish line. When the crowd first spotted Orville and Foulois returning over a distant ridge, car horns began to honk. At 7:08 Orville crossed the line amid more honking of horns and wild cheering.

When the *Flyer* landed, Wilbur raced to congratulate his younger brother—Foulois said it was the first time he had ever seen Wilbur smile. Wilbur had reason to be happy. The pressure was finally off. They had fulfilled the terms of their contract and would receive thirty thousand dollars from the army.

THE FASTEST MAN ALIVE

After Fort Myer the focus of aviation turned to the world's first international air races held in late August at Reims, France. The competition at Reims proved how quickly the rest of the world was catching up with the Wrights. At the beginning of 1908 only ten men in the world had stayed airborne for as long as one minute. At Reims, twenty-two airmen made eighty-seven flights of three miles or more (one pilot flew 111 miles). All the records the Wrights had set in the past year were broken.

American Glenn Curtiss, known as "the fastest man alive," set a speed record of 47.1 miles per hour over a twenty-kilometer course. Although Curtiss was the hero of Reims, that did not stop Wilbur from filing a lawsuit against him for patent infringment at the very same time. Both he and Orville had long believed that Curtiss's system of flight control had been "borrowed" from them.

Since Curtiss disagreed and refused to negotiate for use of their patents, the issue would have to be settled in court. Orville was in Germany with Katharine when the lawsuit was filed. He had gone to Berlin for a series of demonstration flights relating to some German contracts they had re-

Glenn Curtiss set aviation records as the "fastest man alive."

cently signed. Hardly anyone in that part of Europe had ever seen a real airplane and Orville's flights were a sensation.

Crowds as large as two hundred thousand came out to watch him fly. Orville even took Crown Prince Friedrich Wilhelm for a fifteen-minute flight. Also, between August 30 and October 4, Orville recaptured the world records for altitude and duration of flight.

WILBUR'S SPECTACULAR FAREWELL

While Orville was making news in Germany, Wilbur was thrilling millions who had never before seen a flying machine. That fall he accepted an offer of fifteen thousand dollars to appear at a huge two-week celebration in New York Harbor. The Hudson-Fulton Celebration commemorated the 300th anniversary of Henry Hudson's exploration of the area, as well as the 102nd anniversary of Robert Fulton going up the Hudson in a commercial steamboat.

The harbor was filled with ships from all over the world, including forty warships. As part of the festivities, Wilbur had agreed to make either a ten-mile flight or a flight of an hour—plus whatever other flights he could fit in. On September 29 he took off from Governors Island, where a hangar had been specially built for him. He had a red canoe strapped between the skids as a flotation device. Always practical, Wilbur figured that if he got in trouble over water, the canoe could keep the *Flyer* afloat until help arrived.

This first public flight was supposed to just be a short one over the ships in the harbor. But the *Flyer* was handling so well that Wilbur turned and headed for the Statue of Liberty a mile away. As he rounded it at waist level, barely twenty feet away, most observers thought they were witnessing a spectacular crash. When they realized he was demonstrating his control over the machine, ferryboat whistles and ship's horns began sounding excitedly.

Few Americans had ever seen an airplane in flight and, like the French the year before, New Yorkers found the sight of a man controlling a machine in the air

---

"HIGHER, ORVILLE, HIGHER"

May 25, 1910, was a memorable date for several reasons. It marked the only time that Wilbur and Orville ever flew together. They spent most of that day training three new pilots at the Huffman Prairie. Then, toward the end of the afternoon, their eighty-one-year-old father requested a ride. This account is from Tom Crouch's The Bishop's Boys.

"Orville, who was doing all the flying now, went to work immediately. Wilbur stayed with his father, explaining the preparations needed to get the machines safely into the air. They were at it all day. Orville made fourteen flights before dusk, most of them training hops to give the three new men, Frank Coffyn, Art Welsh, and Ralph Johnstone, an opportunity to get the feel of the controls. . . .

Late that afternoon, Wilbur took a seat on the exposed lower wing next to his brother. They circled the field for just over six minutes. It was the only time they would ever fly together, something they had promised their father they would never do. Just this once, for the sake of history, he had relented.

Then it was Milton's turn. The old man had never flown before. The opportunity had always been there—he had simply never asked. Now he climbed up next to his youngest son for the first time. They remained aloft for 6 minutes, 55 seconds, never climbing above 350 feet. Orville had been unnecessarily worried about his father's reaction. At one point during the flight Milton leaned close to his son's ear and shouted above the combined roar of engine, propellers and slipstream: 'Higher, Orville, higher.'"

Wilbur Wright (right) examining the canoe he attached to the Flyer *before performing the first flight over water. Fortunately, he never needed to use it.*

deeply thrilling. The huge luxury liner *Lusitania* happened to be steaming out of the harbor at the very moment Wilbur rounded the Statue of Liberty. Glancing down, Wilbur saw "everywhere on her decks whirlpools of handkerchiefs, hats, umbrellas, and even wraps and coats that the passengers had stripped from their backs and were waving in delirious joy."[98]

A SALUTE TO THE KING

A mighty blast from the foghorn of one of the world's largest ships saluted Wilbur as he flew over, "a salute from the Queen of the water to the King of the air,"[99] is how one reporter described it. All this was observed by at least a half million awestruck people watching from boats, rooftops, shorelines, and parks.

Caught up in the excitement of the moment, the soldiers at Governors Island cheered wildly when Wilbur landed a few moments later. Nonchalant as always, Wilbur had a faint smile on his lips as he climbed out of the *Flyer* and remarked dryly to his mechanic, "Goes pretty well, Charlie."[100]

Wilbur's flight four days later may have been the highlight of his flying career. Without a doubt, it was witnessed by the largest audience ever to see a man fly. Over a million New Yorkers crowded every available inch of viewing space along the shore and on wharves, piers, and rooftops.

At ten o'clock on a bright, sunny Monday morning, Wilbur took off again from Governors Island. With the sound of countless ship's horns and whistles echoing in his ears, he headed north toward the tip of Manhattan. His destination was Grant's Tomb, some ten miles up the Hudson River.

Flying at forty miles an hour, the *Flyer* was knocked sideways by a gust of wind coming from between the tall buildings at Twenty-Third Street, but Wilbur regained control quickly. After he left the city behind, Wilbur dropped down closer to the water to let the thousands of spectators lining the route get a better view.

When he finally reached Grant's Tomb he banked left, crossing over the British warships, *Drake* and *Argyll,* then banked left again to follow the western shore of the Hudson back to Governors Island. Again, as with his circling of the Statue of Liberty, these maneuvers caused the greatest excitement.

As one enthusiastic observer put it, "The most entrancing sight was his turning of the airship for the return flight. The machine seemed to float and run."[101] Those who witnessed the control Wilbur had over his machine that day no longer had the slightest doubt that the age of flight had arrived.

THEIR CREATION OUTGREW THEM

Peter L. Jakab, in Visions of a Flying Machine, *takes a close look at the Wright brothers' process of invention. He notes that by 1910, their major inventions were all behind them.*

"The Wright brothers went on to market their flying machine successfully in 1908 and 1909 with sales and licensing agreements in the United States and Europe. By 1910, they were world celebrities and well on their way to becoming very wealthy men. But, ironically, just as the Wrights began to reap the full fruit of their years of labor, the rest of the aeronautical world was passing them by. The technology that they created almost single-handedly had been embraced by other talented enthusiasts of flight and quickly brought to a level that made Wright aircraft appear primitive even in their own day. The brothers never carried the development of their invention beyond the 1905 airplane in any meaningful way. . . . Nevertheless, it is unfair to criticize Wilbur and Orville for failing to keep pace with the technology to which they had given birth. They had done enough."

9 Masters of the Air

By the end of 1909 the Wright brothers had established themselves as the leading figures in the world of aviation. But darker days lay ahead. A combination of lawsuits, an untimely death, and an ugly feud with the Smithsonian Institution placed a shadow over their achievements. It would be another thirty years or so before that shadow began to lift, allowing the Wright brothers to assume their rightful place as two of the greatest American inventors in history.

The bad feelings toward the Wrights began after they sued Glenn Curtiss at the Reims air show in 1909. They asked the courts to prohibit Curtiss from selling or

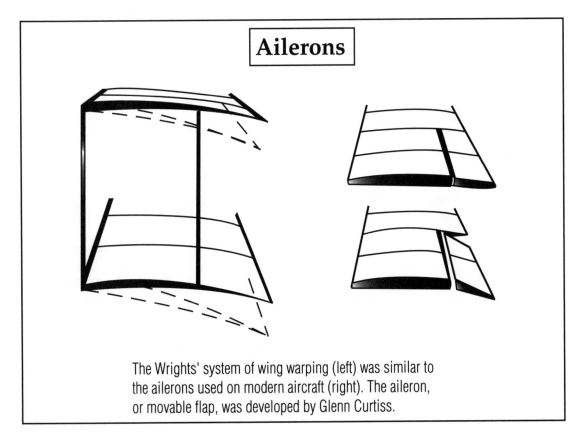

Ailerons

The Wrights' system of wing warping (left) was similar to the ailerons used on modern aircraft (right). The aileron, or movable flap, was developed by Glenn Curtiss.

using flying machines for exhibition purposes until he agreed to pay a licensing fee. Wilbur and Orville contended that Curtiss was controlling his plane with the system of wing warping they had invented.

Even though it seemed to work in much the same way, Curtiss claimed his system was different. Instead of actually twisting the wings as the Wrights did, Curtiss used a movable flap, or "aileron," mounted on the edge of the wing (the same system that is used on all planes today).

In essence, the lawsuit was about whether wing warping was the same as using ailerons. Few people then had the aeronautical knowledge to even understand the difference between wing warping and ailerons—one reason the issue stayed in the courts for so long. But the real question, said critics of the Wrights, was whether a person could patent a basic physical principle. If someone had invented and patented an axle, they asked, could he then collect royalties from anyone who ever used a wheel?

Further complicating matters was the fact that after 1909 there was big money to be made in air shows. The public was hungry to see this marvelous invention in action and did not mind paying for the privilege. Yet Wilbur and Orville did not feel it was right that others were making thousands of dollars from a system *they* had perfected. In an article in *Aeronautics* magazine they described their position:

The Wright Company airplane factory in Dayton, Ohio only made planes for a few years.

A PUBLIC RELATIONS DISASTER

Regardless of the merits of the patent lawsuits, there is no question that they hurt the Wright brothers' image. In The Bishop's Boys *Tom Crouch discusses their possible impact on the growth of American aviation.*

"The Wright-Curtiss feud had become a public relations disaster. While the Wright Company had its defenders, it was increasingly portrayed as a cutthroat organization, determined to smash honest competitors by fair means or foul. The fact that Curtiss continued to prosper throughout the period of the patent suits was generally overlooked. Moreover, there was a growing assumption that the patent suits had retarded the development of American aeronautics, enabling European competitors to forge ahead.

It is impossible to gauge the impact of the patent wars on the growth of aviation in America. Clearly other factors, including government subsidies, prize competitions and international rivalry, provide a full explanation for the rapidity of European advance during 1906–1914. At the most basic level, the situation was proof of the old adage that it is sometimes better to be a fast second. The French, having lost the race for the invention of that airplane, had swept past the Wrights and everyone else by sheer momentum."

When a couple of flying machine inventors fish . . . in waters where hundreds had previously fished for thousands of years in vain, and after risking their lives hundreds of times, and spending years of time and thousands of dollars, finally succeed in making a catch, there are people who think it a pity that the courts should give orders that . . . those who wish to enjoy the feast shall contribute something to pay the fishers.[102]

Not long after the Curtiss lawsuit, the Wright brothers formed a business to build airplanes in Dayton. Wilbur was the president and Orville the vice president. The Wright Company was backed by a group of wealthy businessmen, so the brothers could afford to sue anyone they felt was infringing on their copyright.

But money—especially after 1910—was not the primary reason the brothers insisted on their rights. As the legal battles continued they became increasingly

In June 1912, thousands of mourners gathered for Wilbur Wright's funeral in Dayton, Ohio.

concerned about protecting their reputation as the inventors of the airplane. Courtroom opponents, both in Europe and America, tried to discredit the Wrights by contending that they had not really invented anything original.

Such assertions belittled their accomplishments and made the brothers even more determined to fight. They well remembered the years when everyone thought they were crazy. "It is rather amusing, after having been called fools and fakers for six or eight years," noted an exasperated Wilbur, "to find now that people knew exactly how to fly all the time."[103]

Explaining complex aeronautical issues in a courtroom took months of prep-

aration. Although Wilbur was good at explaining difficult concepts clearly, he would have preferred to be doing aeronautical research. "Only two things lead me to put up with responsibilities and annoyances, . . . " he wrote to Orville. "First, the obligations to people who put money into our business, and second, the reluctance a man normally feels to allow a lot of scoundrels and thieves to steal his patents, subject him to all kinds of troubles or even try to cheat him out of his patents entirely."[104]

But the legal battles took a toll on Wilbur's health. In February and March of 1912 he spent weeks compiling a complete history of the evolution of the airplane for the Curtiss trial. After meetings with his lawyers, he would return home pale and exhausted.

"The amount of his intellectuality, in describing their invention, was marvelous," wrote Milton Wright in his diary. "It must have greatly wearied him."[105] In late April Wilbur fell ill on a trip to Boston to talk with one of his lawyers. Upon his return to Dayton, he felt even worse. At first, the family doctor thought he might have a touch of malaria, but after four days in bed his condition grew worse. It soon became apparent that, like Orville sixteen years earlier, Wilbur had typhoid fever.

Bedridden with a high fever for most of May, Wilbur hung on till the end of the month. He died quietly in his sleep at 3:15 on the morning of May 30. He was just over forty-five years old. In his diary notes for the year, Milton Wright wrote a final epitaph for his son:

> In memory and intellect, there was none like him. He systematized everything. His wit was quick and keen. He could say or write anything he wanted to. He was not very talkative. His temper could hardly be stirred. He wrote much. He could deliver a fine speech, but was modest.[106]

ORVILLE ALONE

Orville was deeply affected by his brother's death. "Probably Orville and Katharine felt the loss the most," noted their father. "They say little."[107] But both Orville and Katharine were bitter. They believed that the men who had forced them into court

Glenn Curtiss—the Wrights' most determined adversary—seated at the wheel of his airplane.

—especially Glenn Curtiss—were partly responsible for Wilbur's death.

In an interview with the *New York Times,* Orville claimed that the Curtiss lawsuit "worried Wilbur, first into a state of chronic nervousness, and then into physical fatigue, which made him easy prey for the typhoid which caused his death."[108] Curtiss declared Orville's charges absurd and accused him of trying to stifle the growth of aviation in America.

Finally, on January 13, 1914, the U.S. Circuit Court of Appeals issued a ruling in favor of the Wright brothers. In granting their claims, the judge stated that the Wrights "may fairly be considered pioneers in the practical art of flying with heavier-than-air machines."[109] Although Orville felt vindicated, Curtiss did not give up.

Since the court ruling applied to the *system* of wing warping and rudder control invented by Wilbur and Orville, he said he would build planes in which the ailerons were not connected to each other. It would make his planes more difficult to fly, but that way the patent might no longer apply. Both he and Orville knew that the argument was weak, but it could still take years for the courts to settle the issue.

In the meantime Curtiss came up with a strategy that incensed the Wrights. He figured that if he could show that another experimenter *could* have flown before December 17, 1903, it might make his patent fight easier.

The only candidate seemed to be Samuel Langley, even though Langley's *Aerodrome* had failed miserably in its only two attempts at flight.

Curtiss was not discouraged. His friend Albert Zahm was director of the Langley Aerodynamical Laboratory at the Smithsonian and had in his possession the remains of the *Aerodrome.* Curtiss and Zahm encouraged the Smithsonian to rebuild the machine.

A SECRET SCHEME

The Smithsonian agreed to the project, stating that they simply wanted to see whether Langley's craft could have flown. But the real reason may have been stated by Glenn Curtiss in a letter to a friend. "I think I can get permission to rebuild the machine, which would go a long way toward showing the Wrights did not invent the flying machine as a whole but only a balancing device, and we would get a better decision next time."[110]

Although the *Aerodrome* was supposed to be returned to its original 1903 condition for the experiment, Curtiss and Zahm secretly modified the shape of the wings and incorporated at least thirty other alternations that helped the craft fly better that it would have in 1903. In May and June of 1914, those changes helped the *Aerodrome* lift a few feet off the surface of a lake near Hammondsport, New York.

Although these "flights" lasted less than five seconds, they were enough for Zahm to claim that the *Aerodrome* "is capable of flying with a pilot and several hundred pounds of useful load. It is the first airplane in history of which this can truthfully be said."[111] Then, instead of listing all the alterations that had been made, he reported that the *Aerodrome* had flown without modifications.

Orville was not the only one who smelled something fishy. Griffith Brewer, an aviation author, wrote a letter to the *New York Times,* asking, "Why, if such a demonstration was decided on, was not some impartial, unprejudiced person chosen to make the tests, instead of the person who had been found guilty of infringement of the Wright patent?"[112]

Even more outrageous from the Wrights' standpoint was the note placed beside the restored 1903 *Aerodrome* when it was put on display at the U.S. National Museum in 1918:

The first man-carrying aeroplane in the history of the world capable of sustained free flight. Invented, built, and tested over the Potomac River by Samuel Pierpont Langley in 1903.

A WISE RULING

World War I finally ended the Wright brothers' patent wars. In the interests of patriotism a licensing agreement among all airplane manufacturers was worked out. Fred E.C. Culick's and Spencer Dunmore's On Great White Wings: The Wright Brothers and the Race for Flight *explains why the Wrights eventually won their legal battles.*

"The confusion and enormous amount of litigation generated by the Wrights' patent was caused by one flaw: nobody involved in the affair—not the Wrights, not other inventors, and certainly not the lawyers—understood the essence of wing warping or the difference between it and ailerons. . . .

The patent battles were waged at great cost ($150,000, Orville estimated), probably broke Wilbur's health, and may have set back aviation in the United States—but the Wrights' patent was upheld. Why?

As Judge Learned Hand asserted, using brilliant reasoning and insight (even though he didn't understand the technical basis of control), it was not a matter of the mechanics—whether warping or ailerons—but of the principle: wing warping while simultaneously using rudders to compensate for adverse yaw.

That was what the Wrights had discovered, and what they were trying to protect. And no amount of modification by anyone else could take that away from them."

Successfully flown in Hammondsport, N.Y., June 2, 1914. [113]

By this time Orville had sold the Wright Company; he had never felt comfortable with the public duties that went with being its president. Fortunately, by then the patent issues with other airplane makers had been worked out to everyone's satisfaction. Because of World War I there was a great need to build more airplanes. In order to resolve the issue once and for all, American airplane manufacturers agreed to pay the Wright Company a one-time fee.

On the other hand, the Smithsonian experiments at Hammondsport were proving more damaging to the Wright brothers' reputation than any court battle. As Orville put it, "Silent truth cannot withstand error aided by continued propaganda." [114]

A CONSTANT REMINDER

As reported in Fred C. Kelly's The Wright Brothers: A Biography Authorized by Orville Wright, *Orville received many letters pleading with him to not send the* Flyer *out of the country. In his replies he expresses regret, but his reasoning turned out to be flawless. In the end, his maneuver accomplished exactly what he had hoped it would.*

"I believe that my course in sending our Kitty Hawk machine to a foreign museum is the only way of correcting the history of the flying machine, which by false and misleading statements has been perverted by the Smithsonian Institution. In its campaign to discredit others in the flying art, the Smithsonian has issued scores of these false and misleading statements. They can be proved to be false and misleading from documents. But the people of today do not take the trouble to examine the evidence.

With this machine in any American museum the national pride would be satisfied; nothing further would be done and the Smithsonian would continue its propaganda. In a foreign museum this machine will be a constant reminder of the reasons for its being there, and after the people and petty jealousies of this day are gone, the historians of the future may examine the evidence impartially and make history accord with it. Your regret that this old machine must leave the country can hardly be so great as my own."

A wooden stand-in for Orville is fitted to the Wright 1903 Flyer *at a Science Museum exhibit in London.*

One magazine hailed Dr. Langley as "Discoverer of the Air" and *L'Aerophile*, the most influential publication devoted to aviation, praised the Smithsonian for doing "justice to a great pioneer."[115] If Orville did not do something soon, it seemed that his and his brother's achievements might be permanently overshadowed. In the spring of 1925, Orville acted. He announced that he would be sending the Wright's 1903 plane to the Science Museum of London.

It turned out to be a brilliant maneuver. He knew that people who had not been following the issue closely would wonder why the Wrights would take such a drastic step. Most Americans considered the Wrights' 1903 plane a national treasure. As long as it remained in a foreign country, they would want it back. When they learned the details of what had really happened, some of them would put pressure on the Smithsonian to admit it had misled the public.

Even so, it was not until 1943 that Charles Abbot, then the secretary of the Smithsonian, agreed to Orville's terms for ending the feud. He would publish the differences between the 1903 *Aerodrome* and the one flown at Hammondsport in 1914, along with an admission that the 1914 Smithsonian report had been misleading.

That was all the apology Orville needed. He began preparations to have the *Flyer* sent to the Smithsonian when World War II ended. Unfortunately, Orville did not live to see that historic aircraft hanging

The 1903 Flyer, *dubbed the "Kitty Hawk," finally went on exhibit at the Smithsonian in December, 1948.*

in the Smithsonian. On January 27, 1948, he suffered a heart attack while trying to fix the doorbell at his home. He died three days later at the age of seventy-seven.

That December, on the forty-fifth anniversary of the first flight, 850 guests attended the presentation of the Wrights' 1903 *Flyer* to the National Museum at the Smithsonian. Milton Wright, a nephew of Wilbur and Orville, represented the family and Vice President Alben Barkley accepted on behalf of the people of the United States.

At last, the Wrights' *Flyer* had come home—a return that helped secure the brothers' place in history. Wilbur and Orville would have heartily approved of the sign posted nearby that evening. In the kind of clear language they would

have appreciated, it matter-of-factly noted their gift to the world:

BY ORIGINAL SCIENTIFIC RESEARCH THE WRIGHT BROTHERS DISCOVERED THE PRINCIPLES OF HUMAN FLIGHT. AS INVENTORS, BUILDERS, AND FLYERS THEY FURTHER DEVELOPED THE AEROPLANE, TAUGHT MAN TO FLY, AND OPENED THE ERA OF AVIATION.[116]

At Orville's funeral eleven months earlier, the pastor had noted that, although Orville was a genius, he was also "a man who was just one of folks like us—middle class, mid-Western American, with simple, devout parents, and simple modest way of life."[117]

In many ways Wilbur and Orville were ordinary young men, yet they had the courage and confidence to persevere when the whole world was telling them their quest was foolish. John Daniels, a lifesaver at the Kill Devil Hills Lifesaving Station in 1903, had little doubt why the Wright brothers succeeded:

It wasn't luck that made them fly: it was hard work and hard common sense; they put their whole heart and soul and all their energy into an idea and they had the faith. Good Lord, I'm a-wondering what all of us could do if we had faith in our ideas and put all our heart and mind and energy into them like those Wright boys did![118]

The Wright brothers' accomplishment has been called the most remarkable single achievement in the history of aviation. It was also one of the most influential inventions ever. Without the airplane's ability to

The Wright Flyer *was placed above* Apollo Eleven *at the Air and Space Museum in Washington, D.C. illustrating the Wright brothers' significant contribution to aeronautics.*

They Saw What Others Did Not

In On Great White Wings, *authors Fred E.C. Culick and Spencer Dunmore summed up the Wright brothers' genius.*

"The Wright brothers' achievement is unparalleled in human endeavor. After they had assembled and flown their frail aircraft, the world was never the same again. Not only did the Wrights solve most of the basic problems associated with manned flight, they also willingly risked life and limb learning to fly and test their own aircraft. They succeeded where so many failed because they saw the problem as a three-stage exercise. First, the provision of a flight-sustaining surface, a wing, or set of wings. Second, a means of propelling the aircraft. Third, a method of balancing and controlling it in flight."

transport people and goods over great distances, the history of the twentieth century would have been entirely different.

Just as important as the airplane itself was the incredible psychological impact it made. When people finally realized that one of mankind's oldest dreams had been achieved, they were stunned and inspired. If man could really fly, then anything might be possible.

John Daniels was the man who snapped the famous photograph of the *Flyer* taking to the air on the morning of December 17, 1903. Almost a quarter century later, he still had vivid memories of that day. In an interview published in Collier's *Weekly* in 1927, he described the enduring thrill of being a witness at the dawn of man-made flight.

I like to think about it now: I like to think about that first airplane the way it sailed off in the air at Kill Devil Hills that morning, as pretty as any bird you ever laid your eyes on. I don't think I ever saw a prettier sight in my life. Its wings and uprights were braced with new and shiny copper piano wires. The sun was shining bright that morning, and the wires just blazed in the sunlight like gold. The machine looked like some big, graceful golden bird sailing off into the wind. [119]

Notes

Introduction: They Gave Us Wings

1. Quoted in Tom Crouch, *The Bishop's Boys*. New York: W.W. Norton &; Co., 1989, p. 137.
2. Quoted in Donald Hall, ed., *The Oxford Book of Children's Verse in America*. New York: Oxford University Press, 1985, p. 99.
3. Quoted in Donald S. Lopez, *Aviation: A Smithsonian Guide*. New York: Macmillan, 1995, p. 22.

Chapter 1: "He Had Much Faith in His Children"

4. Quoted in Crouch, *The Bishop's Boys*, p. 58.
5. Quoted in Orville Wright, *How We Invented the Airplane*. New York: David McKay, 1953, p. 9.
6. Quoted in Marvin W. McFarland, ed., *The Papers of Wilbur and Orville Wright*, vol. 1. New York: McGraw-Hill, 1953, p. v.
7. Quoted in Fred C. Kelly, ed., *Miracle at Kitty Hawk: The Letters of Wilbur and Orville Wright*. New York: Farrar, Straus & Young, 1951, p. 3.
8. Quoted in Crouch, *The Bishop's Boys*, p. 58.
9. Quoted in John Evangelist Walsh, *One Day at Kitty Hawk: The Untold Story of the Wright Brothers*. New York: Thomas Y. Crowell, 1975, p. 15.
10. Kelly, *The Wright Brothers*, p. 14.
11. Quoted in Walsh, *One Day at Kitty Hawk*, p. 16.
12. Quoted in Peter L. Jakab and Rick Young, eds., *The Published Writings of Wilbur and Orville Wright*. Washington: Smithsonian Institution Press, 2000, p. 60.
13. Quoted in Jakab and Young, *The Published Writings of Wilbur and Orville Wright*, p. 61.
14. Quoted in Crouch, *The Bishop's Boys*, p. 96.
15. Quoted in Crouch, *The Bishop's Boys*, p. 77.
16. Quoted in Fred Howard, *Wilbur and Orville: A Biography of the Wright Brothers*. New York: Alfred A. Knopf, 1987, p. 7.

Chapter 2: The Bicycle Builders

17. Quoted in Crouch, *The Bishop's Boys*, p. 98.
18. Quoted in Marvin W. McFarland, ed., *The Papers of Wilbur and Orville Wright*, vol. 2. New York: McGraw-Hill, 1953, p. 696.
19. Quoted in Crouch, *The Bishop's Boys*, pp. 102–3.
20. Quoted in Crouch, *The Bishop's Boys*, p. 103.
21. Quoted in Kelly, *Miracle at Kitty Hawk*, p. 9.
22. Quoted in Crouch, *The Bishop's Boys*, p. 111.
23. Quoted in Crouch, *The Bishop's Boys*, p. 125.
24. Quoted in Harry Combs, *Kill Devil Hill: Discovering the Secret of the Wright Brothers*. Boston: Houghton Mifflin, 1979, p. 54.
25. Quoted in McFarland, *The Papers of Wilbur and Orville Wright*, vol. 1, p. 103.
26. Quoted in McFarland, *The Papers of Wilbur and Orville Wright*, vol. 1, p. 3.
27. Quoted in Lopez, *Aviation*, p. 25.

Chapter 3: An Idea Takes Wing

28. Quoted in Crouch, *The Bishop's Boys*, p. 165.
29. Quoted in Kelly, *Miracle at Kitty Hawk*, pp. 15–16.
30. Quoted in Howard, *Wilbur and Orville*, p. 31.
31. Quoted in Crouch, *The Bishop's Boys*, p. 167.
32. Quoted in Howard, *Wilbur and Orville*, p. 33.
33. Quoted in Crouch, *The Bishop's Boys*, p. 174.
34. Quoted in Howard, *Wilbur and Orville*, p. 38.
35. Quoted in McFarland, *The Papers of Wilbur and Orville Wright*, vol. 1, pp. 15–19.
36. Quoted in Kelly, *Miracle at Kitty Hawk*, p. 25.
37. Quoted in Kelly, *Miracle at Kitty Hawk*, p. 26.

Chapter 4: Flight School

38. Quoted in Jakab and Young, *Published Writings of Wilbur and Orville Wright*, p. 52.
39. Quoted in Jakab and Young, *Published Writings of Wilbur and Orville Wright*, p. 275.
40. Quoted in McFarland, *The Papers of Wilbur and Orville Wright*, vol. 1, p. 26.
41. Quoted in Crouch, *The Bishop's Boys*, p. 190.
42. Quoted in McFarland, *The Papers of Wilbur and Orville Wright*, vol. 1, p. 38.

43. Quoted in McFarland, *The Papers of Wilbur and Orville Wright,* vol. 1, p. 73.

44. Quoted in Crouch, *The Bishop's Boys,* p. 208.

45. Quoted in Fred Culick and Spencer Dunmore, *On Great White Wings: The Wright Brothers and the Race for Flight.* New York: Hyperion, 2001, p. 47.

46. Quoted in Crouch, *The Bishop's Boys,* p. 211.

47. Quoted in Crouch, *The Bishop's Boys,* p. 217.

48. Quoted in Crouch, *The Bishop's Boys,* p. 213.

49. Quoted in Kelly, *Miracle at Kitty Hawk,* p. 44.

50. Quoted in McFarland, *The Papers of Wilbur and Orville Wright,* vol. 1, p. 93.

51. Quoted in Crouch, *The Bishop's Boys,* p. 228.

52. Quoted in Kelly, *Miracle at Kitty Hawk,* p. 81.

Chapter 5: The Whopper Flying Machine

53. Quoted in Crouch, *The Bishop's Boys,* p. 244.

54. Quoted in Crouch, *The Bishop's Boys,* p. 243.

55. Quoted in Culick and Dunmore, *On Great White Wings,* p. 60.

56. Quoted in Culick and Dunmore, *On Great White Wings,* p. 60.

57. Quoted in Kelly, *Miracle at Kitty Hawk,* p. 91.

58. Quoted in Crouch, *The Bishop's Boys,* p. 246.

59. Quoted in McFarland, *The Papers of Wilbur and Orville Wright,* vol. 1, p. 359.

60. Quoted in Lopez, *Aviation,* p. 122.

61. Quoted in Stephen Kirk, *First in Flight: The Wright Brothers in North Carolina.* Winston-Salem, NC: John F. Blair, 1995, p. 192.

62. Quoted in Kirk, *First in Flight,* p. 192.

63. Quoted in McFarland, *The Papers of Wilbur Orville Wright,* vol. 1, p. 364.

64. Quoted in Combs, *Kill Devil Hill,* p. 205.

65. Quoted in Kelly, *Miracle at Kitty Hawk,* p. 114.

66. Quoted in Jakab and Young, *The Published Writings of Wilbur and Orville Wright,* p. 276.

67. Quoted in Walter Bonney, *Prelude to Kitty Hawk.* Hagerstown, MD: Fairchild Engine and Airplane Corporation, 1953, p. 27.

Chapter 6: Pioneers in the Pasture

68. Quoted in Lopez, *Aviation,* p. 32.

69. Quoted in McFarland, *The Papers of Wilbur and Orville Wright,* vol 1, p. 538.

70. Quoted in Crouch, *The Bishop's Boys,* p. 273.

71. Quoted in Kelly, *Miracle at Kitty Hawk,* pp. 130–31.

72. Quoted in Howard, *Wilbur and Orville,* p. 154.

73. Quoted in Crouch, *The Bishop's Boys,* p. 282.

74. Quoted in Walsh, *One Day at Kitty Hawk,* pp. 168–69.

75. Quoted in Kelly, *Miracle at Kitty Hawk,* pp. 136–7.

76. Quoted in Howard, *Wilbur and Orville,* p. 182.

77. Quoted in Howard, *Wilbur and Orville,* p. 193.

78. Quoted in Kelly, *The Miracle at Kitty Hawk,* p. 181.

Chapter 7: The Bird Men of 1908

79. Quoted in Kirk, *First in Flight,* p. 217.

80. Quoted in Kirk, *First in Flight,* p. 218.

81. Quoted in Kirk, *First in Flight,* p. 218.

82. Quoted in Howard, *Wilbur and Orville,* p. 258.

83. Quoted in Combs, *Kill Devil Hill,* p. 281.

84. Quoted in Howard, *Wilbur and Orville,* p. 259.

85. Quoted in Crouch, *The Bishop's Boys,* p. 368.

86. Quoted in Kelly, *The Miracle at Kitty Hawk,* p. 292.

87. Quoted in Kelly, *The Miracle at Kitty Hawk,* p. 311.

88. Quoted in Kelly, *The Miracle at Kitty Hawk,* p. 315.

89. Quoted in Crouch, *The Bishop's Boys,* p. 378.

90. Quoted in Howard, *Wilbur and Orville,* p. 282.

Chapter 8: Fame and Misfortune

91. Quoted in Combs, *Kill Devil Hill,* p. 284.

92. Quoted in McFarland, *The Papers of Wilbur and Orville Wright,* vol. 2, p. 935.

93. Quoted in Kelly, *Miracle at Kitty Hawk,* pp. 310–11.

94. Quoted in Kelly, *Miracle at Kitty Hawk,* p. 323.

95. Quoted in Howard, *Wilbur and Orville,* p. 294.

96. Quoted in Crouch, *The Bishop's Boys,* p. 398.

97. Quoted in Crouch, *The Bishop's Boys,* p. 398.

98. Quoted in Walsh, *One Day at Kitty Hawk,* p. 244.

99. Quoted in Walsh, *One Day at Kitty Hawk,* p. 245.

100. Quoted in Walsh, *One Day at Kitty Hawk*, p. 289.

101. Quoted in Walsh, *One Day at Kitty Hawk*, p. 246.

Chapter 9: Masters of the Air

102. Quoted in Howard, *Wilbur and Orville*, p. 333.

103. Quoted in McFarland, *The Papers of Wilbur and Orville Wright*, vol. 2, p. 1041.

104. Quoted in Kelly, *Miracle at Kitty Hawk*, p. 384.

105. Quoted in McFarland, *The Papers of Wilbur and Orville Wright*, vol. 2, p. 1037.

106. Quoted in Kelly, *Miracle at Kitty Hawk*, p. 388.

107. Quoted in Crouch, *The Bishop's Boys*, p. 450.

108. Quoted in Howard, *Wilbur and Orville*, pp. 393–4.

109. Quoted in Howard, *Wilbur and Orville*, p. 393.

110. Quoted in Howard, *Wilbur and Orville*, pp. 395–6.

111. Quoted in Crouch, *The Bishop's Boys*, p. 487.

112. Quoted in Howard, *Wilbur and Orville*, p. 398.

113. Quoted in Howard, *Wilbur and Orville*, p. 401.

114. Quoted in McFarland, *The Papers of Wilbur and Orville Wright*, vol. 2, p. 1088.

115. Quoted in Crouch, *The Bishop's Boys*, p. 490.

116. Quoted in Crouch, *The Bishop's Boys*, p. 529.

117. Quoted in Crouch, *The Bishop's Boys*, p. 525.

118. Quoted in Jakab and Young, *The Published Writings of Wilbur and Orville Wright*, p. 278.

119. Quoted in Jakab and Young, *The Published Writings of Wilbur and Orville Wright*, p. 277.

For Further Reading

Don Berliner, *Before the Wright Brothers*. Minneapolis: Lerner Publications, 1990. A look at the early investigators who worked to understand flight scientifically. For young adults.

Walter Boyne, Terry Gwynn-Jones, and Valerie Moolman, *How Things Work: Flight*. Alexandria, VA: Time-Life Books, 1990. Offers a clear and thorough explanation of the scientific principles behind flight. Includes many illustrations showing the similarities between birds and airplanes.

Russell Freedman, *The Wright Brothers: How They Invented the Airplane*. New York: Holiday House, 1991. Excellent account of the birth of aviation, with over ninety photos and explanatory diagrams.

Richard M. Haynes, *The Wright Brothers*. Englewood Cliffs, NJ: Silver Burdett, 1991. Readable young adult biography of the Wrights.

Jason Hook, *The Wright Brothers*. New York: Bookwright, 1989. A simplified biography for younger readers.

Donald S. Lopez, *Aviation: A Smithsonian Guide*. New York: Macmillan, 1995. Traces the development of aviation from Leonardo da Vinci to the Stealth Bomber. Interspersed with many color photos from the National Air and Space Museum.

Anna Sproule, *The Wright Brothers: The Birth of Modern Aviation*. Woodbridge, CT: Blackbirch, 1999. A short biography of the Wrights for young readers.

Works Consulted

Walter Bonney, *Prelude to Kitty Hawk.* Hagerstown, MD. Fairchild Engine and Airplane Corporation, 1953. An account of the Wrights' accomplishments issued on the fiftieth anniversary of the first flight.

Walter Boyne, *The Smithsonian Book of Flight.* New York: Orion Books, 1987. Heavily illustrated history of the first eight decades of flight, with particular emphasis on aviation during the World Wars and after.

Harry Combs, *Kill Devil Hill: Discovering the Secret of the Wright Brothers.* Boston: Houghton Mifflin, 1979. A highly enthusiastic account of the Wright brothers' technological genius. Author is a pilot and aviation authority who first flew solo in 1928.

Tom Crouch, *The Bishop's Boys.* New York: W.W. Norton &; Co., 1989. A thorough investigation of the Wright brothers and the early days of flight. Probes deeper than other works into the family dynamics that made their achievements possible.

Fred E. C. Culick and Spencer Dunmore, *On Great White Wings: The Wright Brothers and the Race for Flight.* New York: Hyperion, 2001. Chronicles the triumph of the Wright brothers with easily understood prose and plenty of pictures, both historic and contemporary.

Hendrik de Leeuw, *From Flying Horse to Man in the Moon.* New York: St. Martin's, 1963. Profiles early aviators like Curtiss and Fokker along with many lesser-known figures before moving on into the Space Age.

Benjamin D. Foulois with C.V. Glines, *From the Wright Brothers to the Astronauts; The Memoirs of Benjamin D. Foulois.* New York, McGraw-Hill, 1968. The story of one of the first men trained to fly by the Wrights. Foulois went on to become a major general who headed the U.S. Army Air Corps until 1935.

Elsbeth Freudenthal, *Flight into History: The Wright Brothers and the Air Age.* Norman: University of Oklahoma Press, 1949. A readable account of the Wright brothers' lives, but the author may have been unduly influenced by Albert Zahm, longtime enemy of the Wrights who assisted with the research. Some feel the book minimizes the brothers' achievements.

Donald Hall, ed., *The Oxford Book of Children's Verse in America.* New York: Oxford University Press, 1986. A collection of American poems traditionally enjoyed by young readers.

Charles Harvard Gibbs-Smith, *The Invention of the Aeroplane* (1799–1909). New York: Taplinger, 1966. Traces and analyzes the development of the powered flight. May be a little too thorough for the casual reader.

———, *The Rebirth of European Aviation 1902–1908: A Study of the Wright Brothers' Influence.* London: H.M. Stationery Off., 1974. The Wright brothers helped revitalize European aviation. Gibbs-Smith shows how the Europeans realized much sooner than the Americans the importance of the Wrights' discovery.

James P. Harrison, *Mastering the Sky.* New York: Sarpedon, 1996. Not a complete history, but does a nice job of putting aviation in historical perspective with accounts of some of the major discoveries.

Fred Howard, *Wilbur and Orville: A Biography of the Wright Brothers.* New York: Alfred A.

Knopf, 1987. A comprehensive biography of the Wrights and their times by one of the first researchers given access to the Wilbur and Orville Wright Papers.

Peter L. Jakab, *Visions of a Flying Machine: The Wright Brothers and the Process of Invention.* Washington: Smithsonian Institution Press, 1990. Takes reader through the steps taken by the Wright brothers, showing how they were able to solve technological problems that had baffled the world's best minds.

Peter L. Jakab and Rick Young, eds., *The Published Writings of Wilbur and Orville Wright.* Washington: Smithsonian Institution Press, 2000. Contains over seventy of the brothers' published writings and interviews. Appendix contains fascinating interviews with some of the witnesses to the first flights.

Fred C. Kelly, *The Wright Brothers: A Biography Authorized by Orville Wright.* New York: Harcourt, Brace, 1943. The first true biography of the brothers, although some critics believe that Orville's influence may have prevented Kelly from writing a truly objective book.

————, ed., *Miracle at Kitty Hawk: The Letters of Wilbur and Orville Wright.* New York: Farrar, Straus & Young, 1951. The Library of Congress was given over thirty thousand letters by the Wright family. This collection of six hundred letters is arranged chronologically with commentary by Wright biographer Kelly.

Stephen Kirk, *First in Flight: The Wright Brothers in North Carolina.* Winston-Salem, NC: John F. Blair, 1995. This detailed account of the Wright brothers' experiments at Kitty Hawk focuses on the effect the people and landscape of the Outer Banks had on them. Also describes the largely for- gotten gliding experiments Orville undertook there in 1911.

Donald S. Lopez, *Aviation: A Smithsonian Guide.* New York: Macmillan, 1995. A lavishly illustrated history of aviation and the men and women who dreamed of flight, written by a former World War II fighter pilot.

Marvin W. McFarland, ed., *The Papers of Wilbur and Orville Wright.* Vols. 1 and 2. New York: McGraw-Hill, 1953. Huge compilation of over twelve hundred papers from the collections of Wilbur and Orville Wright and Octave Chanute. As the brothers wished, it allows readers to trace the brothers' thinking in their own words.

Phil Scot, *The Pioneers of Flight: A Documentary History.* Princeton, NJ: Princeton University Press, 1999. Profiles of the men and women who have made major contributions to the world of aviation.

Henry Ladd Smith, *Airways: The History of Commercial Aviation in the United States.* New York: Alfred A. Knopf, 1942. Although it focuses on the growth of the airlines prior to 1942, there is a good account of events surrounding the 1903 Wright brothers' flights.

Norman Smith, *Wings of Feathers, Wings of Flame: The Science and Techology of Aviation,* Boston: Little, Brown & Company, 1972. A review of aviation thought from mythological beings to astronauts.

John Evangelist Walsh, *One Day at Kitty Hawk: The Untold Story of the Wright Brothers.* New York: Thomas Y. Crowell, 1975. Although the author contends that Orville and biographer Fred C. Kelly overstated Orville's contributions to the birth of flight, Walsh may have leaned a bit too far in the other direction.

Peter Wegener, *What Makes Airplanes Fly: History, Science and Application of Aerodynamics*. New York: Springer-Verlag New York, 1997. Contains a thorough scientific analysis of what makes planes fly.

Orville Wright, *How We Invented the Airplane*. New York: David McKay, 1953. A short book describing the Wrights' discoveries in Orville's own words. An illustrated version was published in 1988.

Index

Picture Credits

About the Author

A former editor at *Reminisce* magazine, Michael J. Martin is a freelance writer whose home overlooks the Mississippi River in Lansing, Iowa. His articles have appeared in publications like *Boys' Life, Timeline,* and *American History.* Recent books include a history of skateboarding and another on the Emancipation Proclamation.